For Men Only

The Study of Romans

By: Gary A. Taylor

Table of Contents

Foreword

When God called out and inspired the writers of the New Testament, He did not choose men who had withdrawn from the tough stuff of real everyday life to write behind the isolating walls of monasteries. He spoke through men whose feet were dirty from tramping dusty Roman roads to the far reaches of the empire. He laid His message on the hearts of men whose hands were scarred from grappling with fishing nets or the rough skins and ropes of tent making. He captured the minds of men who had known failure, frustration and loss. He used men who had dared to risk everything to follow Jesus, and who had been paid with stones, shackles and whips.

When He did set apart a man of high religious privilege and exceptional education, He blinded and broke Saul. He humbled and reshaped him until He had at his disposal Paul, a God-schooled servant who said, "The very credentials these people are waving around as something special, I'm tearing up and throwing out with the trash—along with everything else I used to take credit for. And why? Because of Christ. Yes, all the things I once thought were so important are gone from my life. Compared to the high privilege of knowing Christ Jesus as my Master, firsthand, everything I once thought I had going for me is insignificant—dog dung. I've dumped it all in the trash so that I could embrace Christ and be embraced by Him." (Philippians 3:7-9, The Message)

Today, God is still looking for such men. He wants men through whom He can speak clearly and boldly. He is not looking for perfect men, but broken, forgiven and reshaped men. He is not looking for self promoting arrogance or flattery eliciting eloquence. Instead, he is looking for men who know that they are the recipients of His undeserved love; men through whom He can express a passion and compassion for other struggling men.

In Gary Taylor, God has found such a man. In him, He has a man who has experienced great success and great loss; a man of exceptional energy and talent who has been brought to a place of complete dependence on His Lord. Daily, Gary is in the marketplace, negotiating at the conference table and bending his back on the construction site. He is acquainted with adversity and loss. When he speaks to men, he speaks from the experience of having stepped out of his comfort zone and risked everything. When he engages in man-talk with other men, it is born out of his own journey as a follower of Jesus. He burns with a desire to see every man discover and experience a fullness of life in Christ.

It is from this background, and through these eyes and that heart, that Gary has sought to know the mind of Christ in Paul's letter to Roman believers. Week after week, often crushed by extremely difficult business and domestic situations, he allowed God to capture his undivided attention and burn the life lessons of Romans on his heart. The result is this exceptional volume of 65 studies, written by an ordinary man who desires to see God do extraordinary things. These were taught each week by a man who is quick to tell other men what Paul told the believers in Philippi, "Not that I have already obtained it or have already become perfect, but I press on so that I may lay hold of that for which also I was laid hold of by Christ Jesus." (Philippians 3:12, NASB)

Any man or woman will be wise to read these lessons. The professor and pastor will profit from what Gary has written. However, this book is very much for "men only." It has been written that men might discover and be built up in Christ. But, knowing Gary's heart, it is also written that men might be faithful in teaching and helping to build up other men; that they might take personally Paul's plea to young Timothy, "The things which you have heard from me in the presence of many witnesses, entrust these to faithful men who will be able to teach others also." (2 Timothy 2:2, NASB)

Wayne Bristow
Edmond, Oklahoma

Introduction

Please know I have no formal training. My only training has been given to me by the Lord and other people who have invested their lives into mine. These people are my father, my mother, Dr. Wade Akins, Pioneer Missions missionary; Dr. Philip Jett, my former pastor; Dr. David Dockery, President of Union University; Wayne Bristow, founder of Total Life International Ministries; and dozens of missionaries and pastors who have worked with me in over 75 mission trips over the last two decades in four different countries.

After a Maximum Man conference held in Jackson, TN in 2004, I was asked by several laymen to teach a weekly Bible study exclusively for men. The purpose of the study was to bring men of all denominations and all ethnic, social, and economical backgrounds together for an inductive, expository Bible study. For two years I said "no" to the men and the Lord because I felt I was inadequate to accomplish the task. After lots of prayer the Lord gave me peace and clear direction in February 2006. The study originated with the Book of Luke, which took two years to complete the study, learning about the life of Christ.

We started with a small group of men, about 15-20 would attend each week. We took a passage of scripture and examined it from an historical and theological perspective. Generally, I would try to apply the spiritual truths and arrange them into modern-day applications.

The following year we entered into the Book of Acts for one and one-half years. In Acts, we studied the early day Church, the Holy Spirit, and Paul's mission experiences.

Upon completion of Acts, we started a study of the Book of Romans, which took one and one-half years to finalize. In this study, we learned how to live a life in Christ. The study of Romans consisted of 65 short chapters, which make up my notes from the weekly study. My hope and prayer is that laymen would use this as a means to teach other men the basic, fundamental doctrines of Christianity from a layman's perspective.

Most theological writings are written in a language unknown to the average man. Therefore, I have made an attempt to explain spiritual terminology in a simple and understandable language used by most modern day men.

Oftentimes men are turned off by church lingo that, unfortunately, becomes a form of religious conjecture, which only adds to the confusion and lack of understanding. Jesus used simple parables to explain deep theological doctrines. He never spoke words others could not understand. I have tried to utilize the modern day parables to express the theological meaning of key concepts that oftentimes get lost in the teaching of the study of the Bible.

From personal experience I have discovered that every man is struggling with something in his life. Years ago I thought to myself, if only I could be like "So-and-So," I would have it made. Until I discovered that "So-and-So" was struggling too. The fact is that every "So-and-So" struggles with personal life issues. If we, as men, would be more transparent and become more open with ourselves about what's really going on in our lives, I believe God could begin to do a mighty work in and through our lives.

The first step in the growth of a Christian is to recognize that we have a problem that we cannot fix. The person who runs to the door of denial usually self-destructs, at which time God affords him the opportunity to return to Him in time.

Once we see that life is not about us and it's all about the love of God in us, we become radically changed. Our desires become God's desires and at that point, God creates a new identity in us. We become identified with Christ. We struggle to develop a true and authentic relationship with God because we lack a better understanding of the depth of His unconditional and unlimited love.

8

While we want to know the future, it's important to know that God still holds the future. I trust that you will take the time to read through the 65 chapters and allow the power of the Holy Spirit to speak into your life. My prayer is that God will awaken in your spirit a strong confidence that is of Him for His glory.

At the end of the day, the Bible is basically about three things:

1) Knowing and loving God to your fullest;
2) Loving people to their fullest, even those who hate you;
3) Making disciples and training men to become true followers of Christ.

God is looking for men who will lead and stand in the gap for Him. I trust, with the Sprit of the Lord leading your life, you will find this book one that will help develop a deeper understanding of the spiritual truths of God's word.

CHAPTER 1
ARE YOU A SERVANT?
Romans 1:1-7

"Paul, a servant of Christ Jesus, called to be an apostle and set apart for the gospel of God."- Romans 1:1

In our culture today, being a servant is not a cool or highly respected position to hold. Servants are not usually voted as the most popular people in high school. You will never see a servant on the front of a Wheaties cereal box. In the eyes of our culture, servants are viewed as weak, unappealing, and counter-culture misfits. Paul's servanthood shows us what a real man, a true follower of Christ, looks like. Have you thought about what it takes to be a real man? To be a real man requires us to become a servant of Christ.

Paul, the author of Romans, was a very intelligent, humble, articulate, strong, bold leader and was fully committed to the call he felt on his life. The life of Paul is a story of a bold leader who was corrupt with sin, but was saved by God's grace. While he was a Jewish religious Roman leader, he was also the model commander. No job was too big for Paul. However, he was never the same after his conversion experience while on the road to Damascus when God totally rocked his world. His life experiences, his boldness, his courage, and his suffering are all a testimony of the deep intimate relationship he had with his Lord and Savior. His passion and pursuit of God's Spirit, while making an investment in the lives of people, provide us with a road map of how we are to travel this journey called "Life". Paul was a servant of Christ. He made no bones about it. He saw this as a badge of honor. He was not ashamed to lower himself so that Christ could fully shine.

As we journey into the book of Romans, we will see Paul, like a skilled lawyer, present his case for the gospel clearly and forcefully. Paul had a passion for the Church of Rome though he never actually traveled there. The Church of Rome began as a result of Pentecost (Acts 2). As we know, Pentecost was an unbelievable event, which occurred on the festive day when all the Jews came together to celebrate the Day of the Unleavened Bread.

The purpose of Paul's letter was to introduce himself and make a clear declaration of his faith. The Book of Romans is the blueprint for the foundation of the Christian faith. Have you ever asked yourself, "Where do the fundamental doctrines of the Christian faith come from?" For the most part, these doctrines come from Romans.

Romans can be broken into two main sections: Chapters 1-11 – "What to Believe" and Chapters 12-16 – "How to Believe." My goal for this book is to allow the Holy Spirit to show us, through God's Word, the spiritual truths about what to believe as it relates to the gospel of Jesus Christ. It is meant to be a systematic presentation of the Christian faith.

Let's start with the first verse Romans 1:1: *"Paul, a servant of Christ Jesus, called to be an apostle and set apart for the gospel of God."* Paul sums up his attitude about himself in five words: "A servant of Christ Jesus." What do these words mean? To be a servant you must be humble. For Paul, as a Roman citizen, to choose to be a servant was unthinkable. Can you imagine a typical rich, middle-class American being a servant? To be a servant means several things:

1) **To obey**: When a master makes a request what does a servant do? He responds with a good attitude.

2) **To serve**: The purpose of a servant is to serve. In the Christian faith you're not at Burger King – you can't have it your way and serve at the same time.

3) **To depend**: A servant depends on his master for his resources.

Verse 1 convicts us to obey, serve, and depend. Until we have a servant's heart it is difficult to do these things. What is your attitude toward Christ? Your attitude toward Christ determines everything about your life. All of us come into the game of life with a lot of baggage. We all are ridden with the sins of pride, jealousy, and selfishness to the point we are totally blinded by self. There is but one, final answer to this confused and deceived world and it is the love of Christ.

Verse 2: *"The gospel he promised beforehand through his prophets in the Holy Scriptures."* The gospel was prophesied (Genesis 2:3; Isaiah 11:1; Psalm 6:10). One of the elements that make the gospel so powerful is that on many occasions, hundreds of years earlier, God used prophets and His servants to proclaim the future coming of Christ. It's not like Christ just showed up and people started making up how special He was. No, it's much deeper than that. God affirmed what He was going to do and He did it. Show me any other religion whose god foretold what was to happen and it actually happened. This is clear evidence of His divine nature and His divine power.

Verse 3: *"Regarding his Son, who as to His human nature was a descendant of David?"* Paul states that Jesus is the Son of God, the promised Messiah, the resurrected Lord, "a descendant of David." Paul is emphasizing that Jesus had truly fulfilled the Old Testament prediction that the Messiah would come from David's line. By this statement of faith, he acknowledges his position, and declares that he agrees with the teaching of the Scripture and the apostles. Paul outlines the gospel in the following way:

1) Jesus came into the world as a human by natural descent.

2) Jesus was part of the Jewish royal line through David.

3) Jesus died and was raised from the dead.

4) Jesus opened the door for God's grace and kindness to be poured out on us.

The Book of Romans is an expansion of these themes and gives us clear instruction for how to live a life in Christ.

Verse 5: *"Through Him and for His name's sake, we received grace and apostleship to call people from among all the Gentiles to the obedience that comes from faith."* Paul believes that the forgiveness of our sins is "grace." It is an undeserved privilege. Grace is given – not earned. You can't work hard and achieve grace. Grace comes from the entity or person that is in a superior position, as a master to a slave. In our sinful nature we are but men who are depraved. Apart from Christ, we are ugly, no count, unrighteous humans who have the capacity, because of God's grace, to have a relationship with His Son, Jesus Christ.

Will you think about making the same change that Paul made in his life? Servanthood is not natural. It goes against the grain of what is embedded in our DNA as humans. Christ is the game-changer. His love causes us to alter our total way of life. Will you consider counting the cost of becoming a faithful servant and follower of Christ?

CHAPTER 2
HOW DO YOU SERVE GOD?
Romans 1:8-13

"God, whom I serve with my whole heart (or spirit) in preaching the gospel of his Son, is my witness how constantly I remember you."- Romans 1:9

What are you passionate about? Some people are passionate about their families, jobs, hobbies, etc. Paul was passionate about serving Christ. Before he begins his deep theological discussion about the gospel, Paul takes the time to open himself up and ask the Romans to take a look at who he is as a person.

People served the Lord for many different reasons. Paul understood that a person's motives drive them to their real purpose in life. Some serve the Lord out of legalistic effort. Some want to appear to be more moral than they really are. Some serve the Lord out of fear that if they don't, God will punish them. Others serve because of the prestige and esteem that church leadership offers. Some serve because of the peer pressure to conform to certain religious standards. Many young adults serve because they feel pressure from their parents, who may intimidate them and make them feel guilty. Some even serve because they want to make money off of the church. Some see service as a social network or a connection to more business. The question is, "What is the real reason you are serving God?"

To answer this question, we must first realize that all of these different motives are phony and merely external. Regardless of how much service we think we're doing, **Paul tells us clearly that if it's not done out of a sincere, spiritual desire to please and glorify God, it is not acceptable to Him.** 1 Corinthians 10:31 tells us, "So whether you eat or drink or whatever you do, do it all for the glory of God."

15

The dynamics of the Christian life and service are always directed by a person's real, underlying motives. Even when one serves the Lord with the proper motive, but in their own power, there always seems to be the temptation of self-pity when the person's work goes unappreciated. God used Paul because of God's grace and mercy, but also because Paul kept his motives pure. His single purpose in life was to please God. This is exactly what God has designed all of us to do – love, serve, and obey Him, which leads to pleasing Him.

Verse 9 says, *"God whom I serve in my Spirit."* Paul knew that he must be connected to God in Christ before his spirit could be activated. When he gave his life to the Lord, God transformed him into a new person with the capacity to serve God in his spirit. **Without Christ, we cannot serve God in spirit because our spirit is dead or un-activated**. Service is no good without first obtaining the spiritual octane from God to serve. Service in our own power is always negated by human effort. True service requires us to be filled with the Spirit of God. Paul had been a Pharisee, trained and educated in Judaism. He was well aware of how phony the Pharisees were in their worship of God. He lived in the same self-centered environment where most religious leaders were power hungry, self-centered, superficial hypocrites. What is a hypocrite? A hypocrite is anyone who tries to appear more religious than he or she really is. All of us fit this description during certain times in our life journey.

In John 4:23-24, Jesus tells the Samaritan woman at the well, "True worshipers shall worship in Spirit and in truth. God is Spirit and those who worship Him must worship in Spirit and in truth." You see, before Paul became a Christian he had worshipped and served God in an external way ("If anyone else thinks he has reasons to put confidence in the flesh, I have more: circumcised on the eighth day, of the people of Israel, of the tribe of Benjamin, a Hebrew of Hebrews; in regard to the law, a Pharisee; as for zeal, persecuting the church; as for legalistic righteousness, faultless. But whatever was to my profit I now consider loss for the sake of Christ." Philippians 3:4-7).

The key to the Christian life is to have genuine motivation, which means to have an inner desire to serve God for His sake and not our own. We cannot be pressured into it. Pressure causes people to rebel or go the other way. In the same fashion, we cannot be driven by tradition. **We can only be driven by a desire to please the one and only true God**. Paul's life was not about himself and his desires; **it was about following what God wanted him to do**. Paul was a man who allowed the Holy Spirit to lead, guide, and direct his life.

In verses 8-15, Paul's words suggest marks of true, spiritual service. *"First, **I thank** my God through Jesus Christ for all of you, because your faith is being reported all over the world. God, whom I serve with my whole heart in preaching the gospel of His Son, is my witness how constantly **I remember you in my prayers** at all times; and I pray that now at last by God's will the way may be opened for me to come to you. I long to see you so that I may impart to you some spiritual gift to make you strong – that is, that you and I may be mutually encouraged by each other's faith. I do not want you to be unaware, brothers, that I planned many times to come to you (but have been prevented from doing so until now) in order that I might have a harvest among you, just as I have had among the other Gentiles. I am obligated both to Greeks and non-Greeks, both to the wise and the foolish. That is why I am so eager to preach the gospel also to you who are at Rome."* Let's look at the key word in each verse to give us a better understanding of what Paul is trying to communicate:

1) **A thankful spirit** (v. 8): Be appreciative for what God has done for us. All good things come from God. Many times our wants overshadow the blessings God has given us. One day a close friend of mine called and said, "I had a great day yesterday. It was my birthday and my 14-year-old son sang Happy Birthday to me for the first time." His son has multiple sclerosis. He said it was a miracle. This picture puts everything in a more thankful perspective. We often tend to look at the challenges and the negative parts of our life; but in

17

reality, we have more to be thankful for than to complain about.

2) **A concerned spirit** (v. 9): Genuinely care about the welfare of another. Most concerns require us to ask God what we should do. To be truly concerned is an expression of true love.

3) **A willing/submissive spirit** (v. 10a): Recognize God's authority over us and submit ourselves to His leadership.

4) **A loving spirit** (v. 10b): To do anything without love is meaningless. Love is the centerpiece of a Christian life. God's love is unconditional. He never forces His love on us, nor does he ever try to control us.

5) **A humble spirit** (v. 11): To strip away all of our pride and realize how terrible we really are without God. This brings us to a point of humility.

6) **A fruitful spirit** (v. 12): Have a spirit of love and compassion. To be fruitful means to be productive in the eyes of God. God's standards for success are modeled around relationships and character and not financial success.

7) **An obedient spirit** (v. 13): To give ourselves over to the Lord. We cannot love God without being obedient, which means to live according to His standards and not our own. God wants our obedience because that shows our love for Him.

8) **An eager spirit** (v. 14): To develop a passion for following the true purpose of God. A person can follow his own purpose but will not be happy. Every person was designed and created to follow God's plan, which will result in peace. It starts with an eager spirit.

9) **A bold spirit** (v. 15): To have courage to stand up for Christ. Most people will stand up for the right thing, but Paul wants us to take a stand for Christ. Joshua 1:8-9 says, "Keep this Book of the Law always on your lips; meditate on it day and night, so that you may be careful to do everything written in it. Then you will be prosperous and successful. Have I not commanded you? Be strong and courageous. Do not be afraid; do not be discouraged, for the LORD your God will be with you wherever you go." To be bold means to not be scared of what others think. It requires us to be single-minded and purpose-directed, focused on the only thing that really matters – what God thinks. Our motive must be to please Him and this is accomplished through His power and not our own.

Allowing Christ to transform us to obtain the Christ-like spirit that Paul speaks of in this passage is the only way service to God can be accomplished. When we come to the point in our lives that we recognize we cannot get through life on our own and we need God, then we are ready to humble ourselves and give way to His leadership. Will you give yourself so that God can lead you in His way?

CHAPTER 3
LIVING BY FAITH
Romans 1:14-17

"I am not ashamed of the gospel, because it is the power of God for the salvation of everyone who believes: first for the Jew, then for the Gentile."- Romans 1:16

One of my close missionary friends, Wade Akins, has been living by faith for over 40 years. Living by faith not only means trusting in the Lord for the provisions you need, but also trusting in Him to give you strength to take the responsibility to work hard and do your part. This chapter deals with the concept of faith, a word with many meanings. Faith can mean faithfulness. It can mean absolute trust. It can mean confident hope. Hebrews 11:1 tells us, **"Now faith is being sure of what we hope for and certain of what we do not see."** What does Paul mean here in Romans when he speaks of saving faith? Before we try to analyze how Paul is using this word in the passage, it's important for us to understand Paul's passion in life. Paul's passion, since the day he was transformed into a believer on the road to Damascus in Acts 9, was his obligation to spread the gospel of Christ. The central issue of your life is what you believe about Jesus. It's not whether you're Republican or Democrat. It's not what religious denomination you are. It's not whether you're rich or poor. It's about what you believe in the resurrected Christ. This issue defines our relationship with eternity.

Paul gives us a clear perspective of how we should view the world. Let's read beginning with verse 14: *"I am obligated both to Greeks and non-Greeks, both to the wise and the foolish."* What does it mean that Paul considered himself "obligated" to the cause of Christ? Let me ask you a question: How do you feel about your responsibility to Christ? Do you feel a deep sense of commitment or are you just taking God on a test ride? Are you letting God give you a free 30-day trial run and if it works you will stick with it and if it doesn't you'll try something else?

Paul says he is obligated *"both to the wise and the foolish."* The scripture is showing us here that God has given us a clear directive to not just be connected to people who look like us, dress like us, and are our own color. He is letting us know that every one of us is obligated to teach and share the gospel to "all" people. When Paul emptied himself and allowed God to lead his life, he began doing as Jesus did – giving of himself to others to promote the gospel.

Verse 15: *"That is why I am so eager to preach the gospel also to you who are at Rome."* What's your passion? What do you really love doing the most? How much time do you spend watching TV? (The average American spends 14 hours a day watching TV, Facebook, emailing and Twitter). How much time do you spend engaged in learning about God and investing in others? We will always do what we enjoy most. I know my priorities are often misguided. Ask God to change the desires of your heart if you need redirecting.

Verse 16: *"I am not ashamed of the gospel, because it is the power of God for the salvation of everyone who believes: first for the Jew, then for the Gentile."* The gospel's message is life changing; it's powerful and it's for everyone. Paul focuses on God and not his own inadequacies because salvation is for everyone who believes. God called the Jews to be his chosen people (Gen. 12:1-3). Why? Not because *they deserved* to be chosen (Deut. 7:7-8), but because *He desired* to share His love and mercy, teach them, and prepare them for Christ, the Messiah.

Verse 17: *"For in the gospel a righteousness from God is revealed, a righteousness that is by faith from first to last, just as it is written: 'The righteous will live by faith.'"* The gospel shows us how righteous God is in His plan for us to be saved, as well as how we may be made fit for eternal life. After trusting and believing in Christ, it follows that our relationship with God is made right - "first to last." Because of our faith, God declares us righteous. We are not righteous because of anything we have done, but because of what Christ did for us on the cross. **To have faith, we must trust and believe that God is who He says He is and can do what He says He can do**.

Most Christians find it hard to have genuine faith in God. Genuine faith is simply trusting God and allowing the spirit of God to direct our ways in order that His will is done in our lives. Faith is believing that God has the ability and the power to control all things even when we are unable to understand why.

So what is saving faith? It's when man connects directly with God through faith in Christ. Saving faith is supernatural and produces supernatural fruit. Saving faith requires us to die to our flesh and make Christ Lord of our lives. Saving faith is when I give up trying to live on my own and totally surrender all of myself to the leadership of Christ. *"They first gave themselves to the Lord."* II Corinthians 8:5

Are you willing to give God a chance to show you that He is real? Will you live by faith? Will you begin to depend on Him for direction in your life? Will you simply give up and give into His love for you?

CHAPTER 4
GOD'S POWER IS SEEN IN HIS CREATION
Romans 1:18-27

"For since the creation of the world God's invisible qualities—his eternal power and divine nature—have been clearly seen, being understood from what has been made, so that men are without excuse."- Romans 1:20

Let me ask you a question: Why is God angry with sinful people? Because they exchange the truth for a lie ("They exchanged the truth of God for a lie, and worshiped and served created things rather than the Creator – who is forever praised. Amen." Romans 1:25). Sinful people do this because they need to believe in a doctrine of life that supports their lifestyle. **God cannot tolerate sin because His nature is morally perfect**. God cannot ignore you or me willfully rebelling against Him. When we, as humans, reject the truth of God's Word, we are rejecting God. God gets angry when we persist in our sin, because He wants to remove the sin and restore the sinner. We sometimes replace God with a fantasy and live our lives around the fantasy. **All people everywhere deserve God's condemnation of sin.**

Verses 18-20: *"The wrath of God is being revealed from heaven against all the godlessness and wickedness of men who suppress the truth by their wickedness, since what may be known about God is plain to them, because He has made it plain to them. For since the creation of the world God's invisible qualities – His eternal power and divine nature – have been clearly seen, being understood from what has been made, so that men are without excuse."* Does anyone have an excuse for not believing in God? The Bible says no! But would God send someone to hell without hearing the gospel? What happens to the tribesman on the deserted island who has never heard of the gospel? When he dies, where will he go? Paul says that God has revealed Himself plainly to all people through His creation. Unfortunately, people may reject this basic fundamental knowledge of God. People often have an inner sense of God's truth, but they may choose not to accept it. Let me put it this way: <u>People's standards are usually higher than their behavior.</u>

Let's look at another side of the argument. Some people would argue that, if God reveals Himself through nature, why do we need missionaries? My very close friend, Wade Akins, is a missionary and he has provided me with an enormous amount of insight relating to the effectiveness of missions. So, there are several parts to that answer:

1) People will suppress the truth about God, but missionaries provide a Christ-like living example and point them directly to Christ.

2) Missionaries show God's love in a practical way (through things like giving medical aid and supplies, providing food, etc.), thereby persuading the nations to come to Christ.

3) Missionaries convince people of the consequences of their actions.

4) Missionaries help the church obey the Great Commission, which is to make disciples.

5) Missionaries actively tell people about Christ.

Verse 20: *"For since the creation of the world, God's invisible qualities – His eternal power and divine nature – have been clearly seen, being understood from what has been made, so that men are without excuse."* God reveals His divine nature and His personal qualities through His creation. What does nature reveal to us about God? He is a God of might, intelligence, detail, color, and beauty, and a God who controls powerful forces. With the return of Christ, God also provides us an example through which we learn *love* and *forgiveness*. **The fundamental truths of Christianity revolve around the principles of *love* and *forgiveness*.** It is by way of God's love and forgiveness that we are given eternal life. To sum it up, God has revealed Himself both through nature (creation) and His Son (Jesus Christ) so that we may ultimately believe in Him and have fellowship with Him.

Verses 21-23: *"For although they knew God, they neither glorified Him as God nor gave thanks to Him, but their thinking became futile and their foolish hearts were darkened. Although they claimed to be wise, they became fools and exchanged the glory of the immortal God for images made to look like mortal man and birds and animals and reptiles."* How could people who "claimed to be wise" turn to idolatry? Idolatry begins when people reject what they know about God. Instead of looking at God as the sustainer of life, they consider themselves the creator of the universe.

From a psychological perspective, we sometimes project ourselves into things that match our own personal desires that then become our idols. Idols could be our goals, our selfish pursuit of money, power, comfort, or even material items. **Anything that takes the place of or misrepresents God is an idol.** We cannot assign our own image to God, when actually the opposite is true: We were created in His image. Idolatry is when we put our focus and our trust into something created by God. <u>Worship is when our total focus is on God in Christ Jesus.</u>

Here are a few questions to ask yourself: What in your life do you feel you just can't live without: a car, a house, a savings account, etc.? Is there a dream you would do anything to see come true? Does God take first place in your life? Paul outlines the process of falling into idolatry:

1) Reject God.

2) Make up your own ideas about God.

3) Fall into sexual temptation, greed, hatred, deceit, gossip.

4) Grow to hate God and encourage others to do so.

Fortunately, Colossians 3:12-15 shows us how to focus on Christ and live for God day by day: **"Put on then, as God's chosen ones, holy and beloved, compassionate hearts, kindness, humility, meekness, and patience, bearing with one another and, if one has a complaint against another, forgiving each other; as the Lord has forgiven you, so you also must forgive. And above all these put on love, which binds everything together in perfect harmony. And let the peace of Christ rule in your hearts, to which indeed you were called in one body. And be thankful."**

The bottom line is that we are to imitate the attitude of Christ: God forgave us, so we must forgive others. However, we can't do it on our own; therefore, we must let God guide our lives. Let the peace of Christ rule in your heart – love is the greatest virtue ("If I give all I possess to the poor and surrender my body to the flames, but have not love, I gain nothing." 1 Corinthians 13:3). We must love despite differences. Love is not a feeling, but rather an act or decision. Living in love leads to a life of peace. **Trust in Christ to always be able to solve conflict and his peace will rule your life**. ("Whatever you have learned or received or heard from me, or seen in me – put it into practice. And the God of peace will be with you." Philippians 4:9).

Verses 24-25: *"Therefore God gave them over in the sinful desires of their hearts to sexual impurity for the degrading of their bodies with one another. They exchanged the truth of God for a lie, and worshiped and served created things rather than the Creator – who is forever praised. Amen."* When a person rejects God, God allows them to live as they choose. God gives them over to themselves and Satan, allowing them to suffer the natural consequences of their sin.

All sinners must trust Christ in order to put themselves back on the path to recovery. Paul states man's underlying wickedness: **All of us have a sin disease and as we empty ourselves and replace self with Christ we become more ashamed of our sinful nature**. The closer we walk with God the more sin is exposed in our lives. <u>Our identity should be in Christ, not in the things Christ made.</u> Most of us identify ourselves with what we do. As men, we become who we are through our job, families, friends, or other associations we might have. If someone asks you who you are or what you do, most of the time you will explain yourself through the relationship you have with one of these. <u>But our true identity is in Christ.</u>

Does life without God mean freedom? No, freedom can only come as a result of salvation in Christ. Most non-Christians view Christianity as a religion. Religion, to a non-Christian, means just another set of rules and regulations one must abide by. But true freedom was expressed when Christ gave His life so that we would be set free forever. What is the opposite of freedom? Slavery. There is no worse slavery than being a slave to sin. People tend to believe lies that reinforce their own selfish desires and beliefs. <u>Be careful about what you base your convictions upon and know that the Bible is the only standard for truth.</u>

In a way the Christian life is inverted to the world. Before I can be set free from my past and my sin I must become a "slave" to Christ. I must relinquish all of my rights, thoughts, self will over to him before I experience true freedom.

Verses 26-27: *"Because of this, God gave them over to shameful lusts. Even their women exchanged natural relations for unnatural ones. In the same way the men also abandoned natural relations with women and were inflamed with lust for one another. Men committed indecent acts with other men, and received in themselves the due penalty for their perversion."*

29

God has a plan that includes natural sexual relations. **Sin distorts the natural use of God's plan.** Homosexuality is forbidden (Leviticus 18:22). God sets these standards, not society. While our society has allowed the tide to shift into an open door to homosexuality, God still forbids it. As Christians, we are commanded to hate the sin, not the sinner. Many homosexuals are driven by desire. What's worse – homosexuality or cheating on your wife? Both are desire-driven. The bottom line is that we must learn to be led by the spirit therefore controlling our temptations, instead of being controlled by them. The only way we can control them is to be led by the Holy Spirit and be grounded in our relationship with Christ. Will you reconsider your relationship with Christ? Will you seek to have a deeper relationship with Christ?

CHAPTER 5
BOILING the FROG
Romans 1:28-32

"Furthermore, since they did not think it worthwhile to retain the knowledge of God, he gave them over to a depraved mind, to do what ought not to be done."- Romans 1:28

The culture in America is transforming at the speed of light. We are in a time where we are like the frog being boiled: If you take a frog and put him into a pot of boiling water, what will he do? He will jump out. But what if you put him in warm water and gradually turn up the heat? The frog will stay in the pot until he boils to death. This is what's happening to the morals and lifestyles of most Americans today. We are being boiled to death without even knowing it.

In the last chapter we talked about how man was not to worship things made by God, but instead to worship the Creator of the things. Romans 1:28-32 focuses on two of the main issues in our society today: greed and selfishness. Let me put it a different way: Selfish people become greedy people. Selfish people are eaten up with bitterness.

Selfish people have a hard time loving others because it's difficult for them to love themselves. Selfish people always blame someone else for how they feel. Selfish people become consumed with themselves. Selfish people must always have people around them who are as needy as they are. Selfish people manipulate others to accomplish their underlying motives. Selfish people are unforgiving in nature. Selfish people never appear to be in control, but they are in control. If not, they feel very uncomfortable with their environment. Selfish people seek attention; they live in a world that revolves around their feelings. No one else matters. Selfish people become needy people. Selfish people are high-maintenance. The crazy thing about it is that we don't see ourselves that way, which compounds the problem. The fact is all people have a certain degree of selfishness they battle every day. The first step to recovery is to recognize your selfishness and insecurities that keep you from becoming a whole person in Christ.

Oftentimes self causes us to try to compartmentalize God. But there's no way to compartmentalize God. When we try to put Him in a box, guess what? He won't fit. When we try to slip Him into privacy, guess what? God cannot be a secret. In order to live a Christian life, God needs to be a part of every aspect of our lives. Some of us are afraid of what others may say; however, families that pray together influence their children. Families who read the Bible together influence their children. Now we know that most young people will stray away but also, most of the time, they will come back to their original roots. At the core of who we are as humans is a distinct and very unique quality: we all have a soul. We have the capacity to receive or reject God. If we receive Christ, we accept who He is and what He can do. If we reject Christ, we deny our souls His gift of "eternal life." The rejection of Christ leads to death everlasting.

Paul's writing to the Church of Rome gives us a clear view of the world. Let's read verse 26: "Because of this, God gave them over to shameful lusts. Even their women exchanged natural relations for unnatural ones." God's will for creation is for husband and wife to leave their families and become one through sexual intercourse (Genesis 2:24, Matthew19:5, Ephesians 5:31). Any time a man cheats on his wife or has sex with another man he is in direct conflict with creation. The practice of homosexuality produces bitterness, which is the root of most evil. The byproducts of bitterness are a guilty conscience, emotional stress, and depression. What we sow, we will also reap. If we yield to the flesh, we will reap corruption. If we yield to the Spirit, we will reap everlasting life.

Verse 28: *"Furthermore, since they did not think it worthwhile to retain the knowledge of God, He gave them over to a depraved mind, to do what ought not to be done."* – "He gave them over to a depraved mind." In other words, a mind that rejects Christ is a depraved mind. The worst thing that can happen to an intelligent person is to think they are smarter than God – "arrogant." This is a serious form of sin that leads to pride and destruction. <u>Confidence in Christ is real hope.</u> Confidence in self leads to selfishness and arrogance.

Verses 29-31: *"They have become filled with every kind of wickedness, evil, greed and depravity. They are full of envy, murder, strife, deceit and malice. They are gossips, slanderers, God-haters, insolent, arrogant and boastful; they invent ways of doing evil; they disobey their parents; they are senseless, faithless, heartless, and ruthless."* These verses show us that there is a process to evilness. The process begins with *thoughts*. The stuff we allow in our minds produces *attitudes*. The attitudes we develop lead us to take *action*. We will eventually take action on our attitude toward something. There are 21 vices described by Paul in these verses:

1) **Unrighteousness:** Rejecting Christ.

2) **Wickedness:** Getting pleasure out of doing what's wrong.

3) **Greed:** Craving for something, like possessions, until it is obtained.

4) **Depravity:** Evilness or sinfulness in general.

5) **Envy:** Displeasure at seeing someone else have what you want.

6) **Murder:** Envy leads sometimes to murder, as in the examples of Joseph and Jesus.

7) **Strife:** Quarreling about things with a sour attitude.

8) **Deceit:** Tricking someone rather than being completely truthful.

9) **Malice:** Ill-thoughts towards someone else.

10) **Gossip:** The whisper of false statements.

11) **Slander:** The gossipers whisper, the slanderers go public.

12) **Haters of God:** Those who are so full of demonic powers and full of self to the point they have totally rejected God.

13) **Insolence:** Believing you are better than someone else.

14) **Arrogance:** Being full of yourself rather than being full of God.

15) **Boastful:** Those who like to make themselves out to be better than they are.

16) **Inventers of evil:** Those who enjoy destroying good people.

17) **Disobedient to parents:** Those who go against God's plan of following the leadership of their parents.

18) **Senseless:** Those who avoid understanding, as in an unwillingness to listen to God (Matthew 15:16).

19) **Faithless:** Those who are not true to God, making them not true to themselves and untrustworthy.

20) **Loveless:** Without natural affection (it was common for pagans to drown or kill unwanted offspring – much the same as abortion today).

21) **Pitiless:** Those who do not show mercy – ruthless, heartless. As with the example of the Good Samaritan - the robbers stole money and beat up the man, but the priest and

Levite walked right by and were pitiless towards him. All three are viewed the same in God's eyes.

Sin produces sin. Only by God's grace and power and through our desire to honor Him, can we grow into His likeness. God's grace produces holiness. We do not become holy on our own account, but since Christ lives in us, His holiness is shown through us.

There is no way we can live a perfect life but we do serve a perfect God. I have discovered that it's not my ability that God is seeking, it's not even my availability, it's my inability. It's my weakness that he seeks. When I am weak I surrender to self and become able to absorb all that He is. Are you tired of trying to live the Christian life? Are you frustrated and do you struggle with hiding secret sins? It may be time to stop trying and start trusting not in your abilities but in the supernatural power of Christ.

CHAPTER 6
NO ROOM FOR POINTING FINGERS
Romans 2:1-11

"You, therefore, have no excuse, you who pass judgment on someone else, for at whatever point you judge the other, you are condemning yourself, because you who pass judgment do the same things." - Romans 2:1

What would you say if I were to ask you the question, "What is righteous judgment?" In this chapter, we are going to take a close look at what Paul says about God's righteous judgment. Imagine when Paul's letter was read to the Church of Rome… every head was moving up and down when they heard him condemn the idol worshipers, the homosexuals, the perverts, and the violent people. However, when he began to say to them, "You have no excuse. You're just as bad," the religious leaders were probably stunned and upset. This hit them right between the eyes.

Let's read verse 1: *"You, therefore, have no excuse, you who pass judgment on someone else, for at whatever point you judge the other, you are condemning yourself, because you who pass judgment do the same things."* Paul is stressing that nobody is good enough to save himself. He is also saying regardless of your sin, whether you're a murderer or a gossip, you must depend totally on God's grace for salvation. Paul is not trying to argue the degree of sin. He is merely telling us that any sin is enough to lead us to a total dependence on Christ. All of us have sinned and without Christ there is no way to be set free from sin.

Whose sins are the hardest to see? Our own. **Whose sins are easiest to see**? Everyone else's. We need to examine our motives before judging others for Matthew 7:1-2 says, "So in everything, do to others what you would have them do to you, for this sums up the Law and the Prophets." Our human nature almost creates a deniability factor within ourselves. Oftentimes we tend to stretch the truth about ourselves to show ourselves in a better light than is reality. The traits we hate in someone else are often habits we dislike in our own lives. Before we ever criticize anyone, we should stop and closely examine our own life. A person who tears down someone else most of the time has an inner insecurity problem. How we judge others is exactly how God will judge us.

Verse 2: *"Now we know that God's judgment against those who do such things is based on truth."* What is God's judgment based on? Truth. Where does truth come from? Jesus said, "I am the way, the truth and the light." Therefore, truth comes from God's Word and Christ.

Verse 3: *"So when you, a mere man, pass judgment on them and yet do the same things, do you think you will escape God's judgment?"* Can we get away with talking bad about someone and then do the same thing ourselves? No. This verse tells us we cannot escape the judgment of God.

Verse 4: *"Or do you show contempt for the riches of his kindness, tolerance and patience, not realizing that God's kindness leads you toward repentance?"* In His kindness, God holds back on His judgment and always gives us time to repent. **Many times we confuse God's patience with His approval**. We've done something wrong and we've not been punished for it, so we do it again thinking it is okay with God. As Christians we must pray, "God show me my sin. Expose my real motives so I can change and be healed." What God wants us to do is to come clean with Him. We cannot move forward until we repent of our sins to our Lord and Savior. He loves us for who we are and He sees us in our full potential.

Verse 5: *"But because of your stubbornness and your unrepentant heart, you are storing up wrath against yourself for the day of God's wrath, when His righteous judgment will be revealed."* For us to be free from our sinful selves we must allow God to remove our stubborn, unrepentant hearts. How does judgment work? John 12:47-48 says, "As for the person who hears my words but does not keep them, I do not judge him. For I did not come to judge the world, but to save it. There is a Judge for the one who rejects me and does not accept my words; that very word which I spoke will condemn him at the last day." The purpose of Jesus' first mission on earth was not to judge people, but to show them the way to find true salvation and eternal life. When He arrives on His second mission, His main purpose will be to judge people on how they lived on this earth and whether or not they followed Him in obedience. God's Word tells us that on the Day of Judgment those who accept and obey will be raised to eternal life (1 Corinthians 15:51-57). Those who reject Christ and live the way they want to live will face eternal punishment (Revelation 20:11-15).

Verse 6: *"God 'will give to each person according to what he has done.'"* Every person will be judged by what they have done. Some use the excuse that most church members are hypocrites. But God tells us that we will each be judged for our own actions. We should not be focused on others being hypocrites, but instead, we should be focused on the hypocrisy we have in ourselves and do something about it.

Verse 7: *"To those who by persistence in doing good seek glory, honor, and immortality, He will give eternal life."* Paul says those who patiently and persistently seek God's plan certainly will find eternal life. He makes it clear that we are not saved by good deeds; but, when we commit our lives fully, we want to please God and do His will. Therefore, good deeds are a grateful response to what God has done and not a prerequisite for earning His grace.

Verse 8: *"But for those who are self-seeking and who reject the truth and follow evil, there will be wrath and anger."* A self-seeker is a person who wants to get ahead of everybody at the expense of others. For these people, God's wrath is certain.

Verses 9-11: *"There will be trouble and distress for every human being who does evil: first for the Jew, then for the Gentile; but glory, honor and peace for everyone who does good: first for the Jew, then for the Gentile. For God does not show favoritism."*

The evil will be punished, the righteous will be rewarded – God does not base His judgment on favorites. According to the life you're living today, how will you be judged?

CHAPTER 7
IT'S NOT ABOUT WHAT YOU THINK
Romans 2:12-16

"For it is not those who hear the law who are righteous in God's sight, but it is those who obey the law who will be declared righteous."- Romans 2:13

- What keeps us from doing the right thing? Why?
- What's the difference between the Law and grace?
- How does the Law affect you? What about grace?

In today's society, many highly intelligent people form rational ideas about God and religion. Our view of God determines our view of the world. The rules of the world are constantly changing. God uses Paul to outline very clearly how God views our world. In simple terms, Paul says that man's view should line up with God's view. There is no room for your own view. It's not about what you think, but it's all about what God thinks.

Verse 12: *"All who sin apart from the law will also perish apart from the law, and all who sin under the law will be judged by the law."* People are condemned, not for what they don't know, but for what they do with what they do know. 1 Corinthians 9:19-21 shows us that Paul's life involved both freedom and discipline: "Though I am free and belong to no man, I make myself a slave to everyone, to win as many as possible. To the Jews I became like a Jew, to win the Jews. To those under the law I became like one under the law (though I myself am not under the law), so as to win those under the law. To those not having the law I became like one not having the law (though I am not free from God's law but am under Christ's law), so as to win those not having the law." If you're not free and secure in Christ within yourself, it's difficult to be free with people. The objective is to be willing and open to bring others to Christ. Paul's main goal was to glorify God and bring people to Christ. He was careful not to get personally entangled in the philosophical or political views of the day. He remained focused on the single purpose of loving people in Christ.

Verse 13: *"For it is not those who hear the law who are righteous in God's sight, but it is those who obey the law who will be declared righteous."* James 1:19-22 says, "My dear brothers, take note of this: Everyone should be quick to listen, slow to speak and slow to become angry, for man's anger does not bring about the righteous life that God desires. Therefore, get rid of all moral filth and the evil that is so prevalent and humbly accept the word planted in you, which can save you. <u>Do not merely listen to the word, and so deceive yourselves. Do what it says.</u>" Many times, we deceive ourselves when we think just because we've heard a message we've done our duty. The first step is hearing God's Word, and the second step is doing what it says. What God is looking for is obedience. <u>Our declaration to righteousness is obedience.</u>

Verses 14-16: *"Indeed, when Gentiles, who do not have the law, do by nature things required by the law, they are a law for themselves, even though they do not have the law, since they show that the requirements of the law are written on their hearts, their consciences also bearing witness, and their thoughts now accusing, now even defending them. This will take place on the day when God will judge men's secrets through Jesus Christ, as my gospel declares."* The standard has been set and the standard is Christ. If you traveled around the world you would find evidence in every society and culture of God's moral law. Can you admit to yourself and to God that you failed to live up to His standard?

The first step towards getting on the same team as God is recognizing the fact that you have a problem. When we see the problem we have, we can then come to God and seek forgiveness. <u>The power of the gospel is in forgiveness.</u> Our inability to forgive others, at the end of the day, limits our ability to be used of God in the way that he wants to be glorified in us. <u>An unforgiving heart is the absence of the love of Christ.</u>

CHAPTER 8
WE ALL STAND GUILTY BEFORE GOD
Romans 2:17-24

"Now you, if you call yourself a Jew; if you rely on the law and brag about your relationship to God"- Romans 2:17

Romans 2:17-24 tackles the fact that even those who are religious are unworthy before God. Actions speak louder than words. As we have seen in the last few chapters, Paul's letter has provided us with a vital understanding of the power of the gospel. He warned the Gentiles that they would be held accountable for every immoral act and that God's wrath would be unleashed. He said only those who were persistent in living for the Lord and seeking glory would receive eternal life.

Verse 17: *"Now you, if you call yourself a Jew; if you rely on the law and brag about your relationship to God."* Here Paul expands his argument to even the religious leaders. Can you imagine a man preaching to a group of pastors saying, "You're going the wrong direction and I'm here to tell you that what you've been doing all along is not right"? Paul criticizes the church leaders because they have knowledge of God that comes from knowing the Scripture, but they refuse to live by the beliefs they preach. He says this makes them as guilty as the Gentiles. Do you remember the idea we started this book off with? Everyone is a product of the sum total of his or her experiences. Every time we learn something about God or Christ we have a responsibility to share with others – with knowledge comes responsibility. Paul tells the religious leaders that they have the knowledge but have not been responsible with it.

Verse 21: *"You, then, who teach others, do you not teach yourself? You who preach against stealing, do you steal?"* Paul is really saying, "You need to teach *yourselves* the Law – not others."

43

What we do is more important than what we say. It's easy to talk the talk but authentic people walk the walk without letting anyone know it. Our actions are stronger than our words. The church leaders knew the Law so well that they learned how to excuse their convictions, while criticizing others at the same time. Here's the deal – the Law is much more than just a moral minimum standard. It's a guideline for living according to His will. Many times we use possessions to measure success, but the Law is a standard measuring stick that guides us to submitting ourselves to the Lordship of Christ. When we realize we cannot live the Christian life without his power we discover the Law points us to Christ.

Verses 22-23: *"You who say that people should not commit adultery, do you commit adultery? You who abhor idols, do you rob temples? You who brag about the law, do you dishonor God by breaking the law?"* In these verses, Paul is trying to relay to the Jews that just because they are of the bloodline of Christ and His chosen people, there's more to the Law than just knowing it. In the same way, Christians today are guilty of the same thing. We can tell you every way to not do something, but ask a Christian how to live an abundant life for Christ and he'll look at you like he just saw Elvis Presley come alive. Why? Because oftentimes we view tradition as equally important as obedience and that's hogwash. Not because I say so, but because God says so. There is no way you can please God without a proper relationship with Him. There is just one real connection to God and that's through Christ. Before we can truly connect with ourselves and truly love ourselves, we must realize the power of love in Christ and understand that our true identity is in Him.

Here's the bottom line: It's much easier to tell others how to live their lives than to focus on living an obedient life ourselves. We can all say the right words, but does that lead us to take action and make a change? **Without change, behavior patterns are set**. God is looking for two things from His followers: Those who will allow Christ to live in them so they can say the right words and also allow Christ to live in them so they can live by those words.

44

Verse 24: *"As it is written: 'God's name is blasphemed among the Gentiles because of you."* **If we claim to be one of God's people, our life should reflect what God is like.** When we disobey God, we dishonor Him. What we do, where we go, who we talk to, and what we say – **it all adds up to who we are.**

Does your life reflect Christ? What are some areas of your life you would like to give to Christ?

CHAPTER 9
OBEDIENCE IS MORE IMPORTANT THAN TRADITION
Romans 2:25-29

"A man is not a Jew if he is only one outwardly, nor is circumcision merely outward and physical. No, a man is a Jew if he is one inwardly; and circumcision is circumcision of the heart, by the Spirit, not by the written code. Such a man's praise is not from men, but from God."- Romans 2:28-29

This chapter hits us at the heart of modern day religion, because all religions follow a certain set of traditions. For example, one of the critical traditions followed by the Jews is circumcision. I want you to take a few minutes here to think about three traditions that you feel are important to your church. A tradition is anything that is done routinely in church that has significance (i.e. bulletins, Sunday service, music, order of service, dress-code, Lord's supper, etc.). With these verses, Paul utterly crushes our thinking regarding traditions.

Verse 25: *"Circumcision has value if you observe the Law, but if you break the Law you have become as though you had not been circumcised."* Circumcision refers to the sign of God's special covenant with His people. Circumcision was a requirement of all Jewish males (Genesis 17:9-14). According to Paul, being a Jew, or being circumcised, meant nothing if the person didn't obey God's Law. On the other hand, the Gentiles, the uncircumcised, could receive God's love and approval if they kept the Law's requirements. Paul goes on to explain that a "real" Jew, one who pleases God, is not necessarily someone who has been circumcised (a Jew "outwardly"), but someone whose heart is right with God and obeys Him (a Jew "inwardly"). Here's the deal: God is looking for and inviting people to make an inward change so that they can become real men or women outwardly by allowing God to cut away all the pride from their hearts.

Verse 28-29: *"A man is not a Jew if he is only one outwardly, nor is circumcision merely outward and physical. No, a man is a Jew if he is one inwardly; and circumcision is circumcision of the heart, by the Spirit, not by the written code. Such a man's praise is not from men, but from God."* Paul is saying that the Jewish tradition of circumcision is not a requirement for being a Christian. We are required only to trust in Christ in repentant faith. He is trying to hammer home the point that anyone whose heart is right with God is a "real Jew." He makes it clear that being a part of God's family is based on internal, not external, qualities. In other words, just because your grandfather is wealthy and has a good name does not guarantee you a free pass to heaven.

Let's go to Galatians 3:6-9 where Paul gives it to us straight up. "Consider Abraham: 'He believed God, and it was credited to him as righteousness.' Understand, then, that those who believe are children of Abraham. The Scripture foresaw that God would justify the Gentiles by faith, and announced the gospel in advance to Abraham: 'All nations will be blessed through you.' So those who have faith are blessed along with Abraham, the man of faith." You see the Jewish leaders' traditions had them trapped. They could not grasp the idea that a person could become a believer without first becoming a Jew and following the traditions of a Jew. But, Paul tells them that from the very beginning man was not saved by the Law but by faith – "Abram believed the Lord, and he credited it to him as righteousness" (Genesis. 15:6). Paul shows us that a right relationship with God is based on faith, which we talked about in chapter 3. **Faith is the heartfelt inner confidence we have that God is who He says He is and can do what He says He can do.** When we really trust in that, then our relationship with God is based on faith.

Here comes the meat and potatoes of this whole chapter. Just because you go to church, sing in the choir, read your Bible and do your weekly Sunday school lessons does not mean you've made the cut for God's team. Just like circumcision, all these church "traditions" do not make us righteous before God. God wants a sincere devotion and obedience (Deuteronomy 10:1-6). He essentially wants to circumcise our hearts by cutting away all our selfish desires and implanting a new desire for Him and His will. Have you ever asked yourself, "What does God expect of me?" God expects five fundamental things from all believers:

1) **Respect God:** Fear Him. Don't be afraid of Him, but respect Him out of love and reverence.

2) **Follow God:** Be led by the presence of His Holy Spirit (read, pray, meditate, and grow).

3) **Love God:** The Bible teaches we can measure our love by our obedience.

4) **Serve God:** Serve Him 100% - not just on Sundays. To serve means to be humble and willing to be led by His Spirit.

5) **Obey God:** Live what you learn; follow the standards given to us by Christ.

When you are frustrated and find it hard to get focused, put these 5 principles to practice and you will begin to find true peace.

CHAPTER 10
GOD'S FAITHFULNESS
Romans 3:1-8

"But if our unrighteousness brings out God's righteousness more clearly, what shall we say? That God is unjust in bringing his wrath on us? (I am using a human argument.)"- Romans 3:5

In this chapter we will see Paul tear down all the common excuses people give when it comes to being sinful. The interesting thing about Paul's day, 2,000 years ago, and today is that nothing has really changed. There are many different excuses that people come up with to justify their position with God, but let me outline a few:

1) I don't think there is a God, so I follow my own conscience. (Romans 1:18-32)

2) I'm not as bad as other people. (Romans 2:1-16)

3) I go to church so I'm okay. (Romans 2:17-29)

So far, in the first two chapters of Romans, Paul has outlined how sin affects every person's life. Here's the bottom line: **No one is exempt from sin.** We all must accept the fact that, without Christ, we are sinners before God. Only when we get to this point can we understand and receive the gift of salvation.

Let's read verse 1: *"What advantage, then, is there in being a Jew, or what value is there in circumcision?"* Here, Paul paints a very depressing picture. He says all of us are pagan Gentiles, humanitarians, and religious people who are condemned by our own actions. God gave us the Law to expose the evilness of mankind for public view. Is there any hope for the world? Is there any hope for you and me? Paul tells us there is.

Here's how it plays out: The Law condemns us because we are unable to live up to the Law. We will never be able to follow the Law 100%. That's true, but here's the key: Our hope in life is not based on the Law. Our hope in life is based on faith in **Christ**. Because of God's love for us, He gave us Christ and we are made righteous in Him. You and I are put right with God because of God's love being expressed through His only Son, Jesus Christ. **We receive salvation, not through Law, but through faith in Jesus Christ**. There is nothing we can do to earn salvation. We can only accept it in faith as a gift directly from our heavenly Father.

Verse 2: *"Much in every way! First of all, they have been entrusted with the very words of God."* Luke 12:48 says, "From those who have been given much, much will be expected." The Jewish nation had many advantages:

1) They were God's chosen people.

2) God chose for Christ to be born through their race.

3) They were the beneficiaries of covenants with God Himself.

However, these privileges did not make them better than everyone else. They actually had more responsibility to live up to God's requirements. As Christians, we must be careful not to embrace the same kind of attitude towards those who are not believers. Sometimes we find ourselves being self-righteous, which destroys our witness. With sharp words we send the signal to others of our self righteous attitude.

Verses 5-8: *"But if our unrighteousness brings out God's righteousness more clearly, what shall we say? That God is unjust in bringing his wrath on us? (I am using a human argument.)"* Many people in the church today assume that if they just say yes to Christ they can turn around and live their life any way they want. They think of God as an insurance policy for their salvation. Some of the most sinful people today are actually in church. Why? Because they make the following arguments:

1) It's God's "job" to forgive.

2) God is so loving He won't judge us.

3) Sin is not that bad. It gives us experiences and teaches us what not to do.

4) It's okay to live the way our culture lives.

What Paul is saying in these verses is, **"Regardless of any of your excuses, every sin will be exposed and dealt with."** As we know, Jesus came the first time as our Savior. He will return the second time as our Judge.

CHAPTER 11
NO ONE IS RIGHTEOUS WITHOUT CHRIST
Romans 3:8-20 (Eph. 2:1-3)

"Now we know that whatever the law says, it says to those who are under the law, so that every mouth may be silenced and the whole world held accountable to God."- Romans 3:19

      In the last chapter we discussed in detail the faithfulness of God and how Christ is the only way to true salvation. I want to start this chapter with the verses of Scripture that support the plan of salvation as outlined in the Book of Romans:

Romans 3:23	Everyone has sinned – We are all sinners without Christ.
Romans 6:23	The penalty for sin is death – We are all bound for Hell without Christ.
Romans 5:8	Jesus Christ died for our sins – He paid the price so we could be set free.
Romans 10:8-10	To be forgiven of our sin, we must believe and confess that Jesus is Lord. Salvation comes only through Christ alone by faith alone. Only Jesus can save.

      Paul begins these verses with a very pointed question, "What then, are we any better?" What is Paul asking? In chapters 1 and 2 of Romans, Paul outlines in detail how it is an abomination when homosexuals, perverts, and anyone outside the institution of marriage have sexual relations. In other words, it is outright sin! He goes on to admonish the Gentiles, then the Jewish leaders in Romans, chapter 3. Now he brings the focus directly to himself and all the Christian followers. What he is really asking in today's terms is, "Are we better than other people?" This is a fundamentally sound question. The way you answer it speaks directly to where your heart is. Here's the issue: A lot of Christians have the wrong view of themselves as it relates to the rest of the world. Paul uses this as an opportunity to remind Christians that we too belong to the sin-laden, guilt-burdened human race. There's no way we can escape the affliction of sin. Just because you have come to Christ does not mean that you are a better person than someone else. **Your increase in righteousness is not because of you, but because of Christ living in you.**

Let's turn to Ephesians 2:1-3. Verses 1-2: *"As for you, you were dead in your transgressions and sins, in which you used to live when you followed the ways of this world and of the ruler of the kingdom of the air,* ***the spirit who is now at work in those who are disobedient."*** – **"The spirit is at work in those who are disobedient."** I have two questions: Who is the spirit in this verse? What is the spirit doing? Let me explain. There are two types of spirits: evil and holy. "The ruler of the air." Which spirit is this? Evil. **All evil spirits are produced by Satan.** What does the name "Satan" mean? **Accuser.** Satan's primary purpose is to accuse you. In Ephesians 4:27, he is also called the **"devil"** – **"and do not give the devil a foothold."** Paul paints a picture of Satan ruling this evil spiritual kingdom along with his demons. Satan is the temporary ruler over this earth. Satan has limited power. Jesus is the permanent ruler and His power is unlimited. Satan may win many battles on earth, **but Christ is guaranteed to win the war and destroy Satan in the end.**

Verse 3*: "All of us also lived among them at one time, gratifying the cravings of our sinful nature and following its desires and thoughts. Like the rest, we were by nature objects of wrath."* Here's the point: All people have a sinful nature. In other words, all of us have a sin disease. We are totally lost in sin and there's no man who can save himself. Can man do well without

56

God? Sure, but God's standard is absolute. Paul clearly outlines for us that no one can be good enough to earn salvation. If we reject Christ, we become, as verse 3 says, "the objects of wrath." In other words, God's wrath will be on our lives. However, if we receive the gift of eternal salvation we will be united with Christ in His perfect life and become good in the eyes of God.

Let me ask you a question: If I gave you a gift, what would be the appropriate response? "Thank you" – an appreciative and grateful response. Many Christians can't just say thanks to God for the free gift of salvation. Often they feel a need to work their way to salvation. **We are only saved by grace through faith, but out of gratitude for this free gift we should seek to serve others with kindness, love, and gentleness.** There is no place for "self" in the Christian life. You see, Christ is not our Savior for our benefit. We are saved for His benefit and for His service so that we can grow His kingdom. Here's the way I look at it: Every Christian will be judged, by what they say and by what they do, **so my ultimate objective in life is to do three key things:**

1) **Love God.**

2) **Love people.**

3) **Make disciples.**

These are the three principles for all Christians to embrace and intentionally make a priority in their lives. Now, let's go back to Romans 3:9-20.

Verse 19: *"We know that whatever the law says, it says to those who are under the Law, so that every mouth may be silenced and the whole world held accountable to God."* This verse asks the question, "What sin do you have in your life that is keeping you from having a close walk with the Lord?" God wants us to do these **five** things:

1) Come clean before God. Admit the sin in your life.

2) Commit to read and grow in God's Word, the Bible, each day. Meditate on God's Word.

3) Commit to pray and ask God for help and thank Him for every blessing.

4) Fellowship with a group of believers who will encourage and strengthen you.

5) Extend your love to others through service. Become the hands and feet of Christ.

The following quotes come from Adrian Rogers' book, Adrianisms:
- The Bible is God's love letter to His children.
- The Bible addresses one problem – **sin**.
- The Bible has one villain – **Satan**.
- The Bible has one hero – **Jesus**.
- The Bible has one purpose – **to glorify God**.

"The more of the Word of God you give away the more it will stick to you."

"How many of you want more faith? Get into God's Word."

"When it comes to prayer it should be our first thought and not our last resort."

"Have you ever said to yourself, 'I don't feel like prayer'? If there's ever a time you need to pray it's when you don't feel like it. Pray until you do feel like praying."

"Your spiritual life will never rise above your prayer life."

"When you pray, don't give God instructions, just report for duty."

"Prayer is the greatest Christian privilege."

CHAPTER 12
RIGHTEOUSNESS THROUGH FAITH
Romans 3:21-26

"This righteousness from God comes through faith in Jesus Christ to all who believe. There is no difference." - Romans 3:22

As we've previously discussed, Paul wrote the book of Romans as an organized and carefully presented statement of his faith to the Church of Rome. So far, Paul has used the letter to do three things:

1) Present the facts of the gospel. (1:3)

2) Declare to the people his commitment to follow the gospel. (1:16-17)

3) Build the case of the "lostness" of mankind. (1:18-3:20)

This chapter will open up a fourth section of Romans, where Paul presents the Good News – the gospel message. For the last eleven chapters we have learned that all men are sinners before God. Every man needs salvation in Christ because no one can fulfill the Law completely. Every person has the sin disease. Paul spends two chapters telling us that we are totally and completely guilty before God because of our sin. Now, Paul gives us the wonderful news: There is one way to be declared not guilty.

Let's read verse 21: *"But now a righteousness from God, apart from law, has been made known, to which the Law and the Prophets testify."* – "Apart from the Law (Old Testament) God's righteousness has been revealed." How was it revealed? Through the Law and the Prophets. The Bible is basically organized in themes:

1) The Old Testament tells of the **coming of Christ**.

2) The four New Testament Gospels tell of **the birth, life, death, and resurrection of Christ**.

3) The letters from Paul and the apostles tell about **how to live for Christ**.

4) The Book of Revelations tells us about **the second coming of Christ**. Notice that the focus of the Bible is on Christ.

Verse 22: *"This righteousness from God comes through faith in Jesus Christ to all who believe. There is no difference."* We are all guilty before God, but faith in Christ produces righteousness to all who believe. When we trust Christ to save us from our sins it really means that we are putting our full confidence in Him to forgive our sins and put us right with the one and only Holy God. **He wants to transform us by empowering us to live by His Word and be guided by His Holy Spirit.**

Verse 23: *"For all have sinned and fall short of the glory of God."* Every person has sinned. Sin causes us to be disconnected from God and leads to spiritual death. We cannot stay alive spiritually without a direct connection with God through Christ. Coming clean with our sin before God is a requirement before we can ever make the cut for God's team. The first step of faith is the most difficult because it requires us to admit we cannot make it on our own and admit the sin we have in our life. People with material wealth find it hard to see themselves in a position of need. In this way, it is difficult for wealthy people to follow Christ (Mark 10:25).

Verse 24: *"And are justified freely by his grace through the redemption that came by Christ Jesus."* What does it mean to be "justified?" **It means to be declared "not guilty."** If a judge declares you "not guilty," what happens? It is as if you have never been accused. **In simple terms, this verse means we are not**

guilty by God's grace. Our sins are wiped clean. What does it mean to be redeemed? **Redemption is when a price is paid.** The term comes from a person being redeemed by another person from slavery. In the Old Testament days if you could not pay your debts you could be sold into slavery to pay off your debtor. The Law provided a redemption clause, which allowed the next of kin to pay off the debt and buy the freedom of the person being redeemed. **God's plan of redemption for us is through His Son, Jesus Christ.** We are justified (declared "not guilty") by His grace (unmerited favor) through the redemption (the payment of our sins) that came by Jesus Christ. All we have to do is simply accept the free gift of salvation and believe that Christ is Lord by trusting Him, and salvation is freely given.

How then are we saved? **It is by God's grace and our faith in Him that saves us. He does the saving.** Ephesians 2:8 says, "For it is by grace you have been saved, through faith – and this not from yourselves, it is the gift of God." What is grace? **Grace is something we can't earn or deserve – it is God's unmerited favor towards us.** Grace is what God does for me. Law is what I attempt to do for God.

Let's go back to how the saving part works. Think of salvation in this way: I do not know how to swim. I'm in a boat with a group of people and I trip and fall out of the boat into deep water without a life jacket connected to me. What will I do? The logical thing to do is to try to swim, but what will happen? Eventually I will sink and drown. I'm in a position of helplessness. In other words, there's no way for me to save myself. The harder I try to swim, the deeper I go under. If I simply ask for help and trust the person in the boat to pull me into the boat, I can be saved. Here's my point: We are all sinners drowning in sin and there's nothing we can do to save ourselves. But God has provided us with a Savior to pull us out of our potential spiritual death. All we have to do is trust Him. John 5:24 says, "Whoever hears my Word and believes has eternal life. He has crossed over from death to life."

What is **eternal life**? **It is living forever with God.** At the very moment we accept Christ as our Savior new life begins. In this way, eternal life begins when one becomes a new believer in Christ. Most Christians think eternal life starts when a believer dies, but John 17:3, says, "Now this is eternal life: that they may know you, the only true God, and Jesus Christ, whom you have sent." The Greek word "know" means "to have an intimate relationship with." Therefore, when we have a deep, intimate relationship with God in Christ, we have eternal life. So when we receive Christ, it becomes a completed transaction. Unless Christ returns before we die, there will be a physical death. Our body will die but our soul will be resurrected and live for eternity when Christ returns. 1 Corinthians 1:15 says, "So no one can say that you were baptized into my name."

Verse 25: *"God presented him as a sacrifice of atonement, through faith in his blood. He did this to demonstrate his justice, because in his forbearance he had left the sins committed beforehand unpunished."* **Christ is our "sacrifice of atonement."** In other words, He died in our place for our sins. God declares Christ's death to be the appropriate designated sacrifice for our sins. The penalty for sin is what? Death. So, God put Christ in our place to die so that we might live. This is the perfect sacrifice. Our sins are atoned for by His sacrifice, which brings deliverance and freedom to us that is not possible any other way. I trust you will study these terms in this chapter several times so that you may grasp the simple, but profound concepts of the doctrine of salvation. The love of Christ is found in His righteousness.

CHAPTER 13
JUSTIFICATION BY FAITH
Romans 3:27-31

"For we maintain that a man is justified by faith apart from observing the law." - Romans 3:28

We discovered in the last chapter the definitions of: **Grace** – unmerited favor. You can't earn it, nor do you deserve it. Grace is what God does for me. **Redemption** – the price paid for freedom. **Justification** – when we are declared "not guilty" before God. **Atonement** – when Christ died in our place. We also learned that the entire human race is completely unrighteous before a Holy God. Therefore, the only thing God could do to satisfy His own standards of righteousness was to offer His only Son as a sacrifice for the sins of all mankind. If we say to God in faith, "God, I believe You are who You say You are and can do what You say You can do," then we recognize who is really righteous. It's God. When we truly believe, God sets us free from the bondage of sin. Everyone is carrying some kind of baggage that gets heavy at certain times in their lives - poor relationships with family or friends, job loss, drugs, alcohol, pride, financial problems, and so on. **Regardless of who you are, everyone is dealing with some issue that, at times, seems bigger than you can handle.**

This lesson deals with justification by faith. Justification means to be declared "not guilty" by faith, acknowledging that God's plan of salvation is the only one that saves. Okay, let's break it down. Was a sacrifice required? Yes. By whom? God. Why God? Because He is the only one who could initiate the sacrifice. **You see, the initiator of the sacrifice is the only one who can declare the sinner "not guilty," or justified through faith in Christ.**

Let's read verse 27: *"Where, then, is boasting? It is excluded. On what principle? On that of observing the Law? No, but on that of faith."* Here Paul is really saying, "If I give you a gift you can't boast about what you did to receive that gift; you just simply say, 'thank you.'" **Faith is simply saying yes to God's gift of redemption and being declared "not guilty," resulting in freedom.** By saying yes we are saying, "God I believe in You. I believe You can do what You say You can do and I believe that You are who You say You are." Faith is when we truly believe God is real. Here's the question: Do you really, truly believe God is real? If not, I challenge you to consider beginning an expedition of discovering who God really is, not because I say He is real, but because you experience who He really is in your own life. **You will never get to know God until you take ownership of your own personal relationship with Him.**

Verse 28: *"For we maintain that a man is justified by faith apart from observing the Law."* The greatest lie in the world, which is made by some religions, is that by doing certain things humans can make themselves acceptable to God. So, if it's not works or good deeds that save us then what does? Paul tells us that we are declared "not guilty" when we simply say yes to the freedom from sin that God offers us through Christ. Let's look at what can't save us:

1) **Morality**: A person who is outwardly moral, many times, loves himself and his morality is used to serve his own self-interest. Just because someone is a "good person" in the eyes of others doesn't mean they are "good" before God; we are **all** sinners, no matter how good, nice, kind, giving, etc. we might think we are.

2) **Knowledge of the Bible**: Like the Jewish leaders, we can know about God and study the Bible our whole lives, but if we do not obey the biblical truths and live out our faith, we will not and cannot be saved.

3) **Going to Church:** Many people think that if they fulfill their weekly "duty" of attending church then God will give them a free pass into heaven.

4) **Active Ministry:** Judas was an active minister, yet was also the one who betrayed Jesus. Your involvement in mission trips, Bible study groups, and other humanitarian projects does not save you.

5) **Conviction of Sin in Your Life:** Just trying to rid our lives of sin is not proof of a saving faith. We can get rid of sin on our own, and when it's not replaced with Christ, more sin can come into our life when Satan finds it empty.

6) **Assurance of Salvation:** Just because we feel like we've been saved, does it make us saved? No. The Bible warns us about people who think they are saved but are not. (James 1:22)

7) **Experience of a Past Decision:** If there is no evidence of godly living in the present, then you may want to reexamine if you really *were* saved in the past. No matter how strong your decision seemed at the time, it's not necessarily proof of salvation if you are presently rebelling against God.

Now let's look at proof that we *have* been saved:

1) **Loving God:** A person with a saving faith will always love God. (Romans 8:7)

2) **Repentant of Sin and Hating the Sin:** A person who loves God will have a built-in hatred of sin. True repentance is confessing, forsaking, and completely turning away from sin. When God touches our lives, our hearts should be broken over our sin. If we sin and it does not bother us that means we are not convicted of it.

3) **Having Genuine Humility:** A person cannot be saved as long as he trusts in himself and exalts himself.

4) **Devotion to God's Glory:** Paul says in Philippians 1:20-21, "As it is my eager expectation and hope that I will not be at all ashamed, but that with full courage now as always Christ will be honored in my body, whether by life or by death. For to me to live is Christ, and to die is gain." Our pride causes us to want recognition and glory for ourselves, but we must realize that everything we have in life are gifts from God. He should receive **all** the glory, not us.

5) **Faith is Prayer:** The heart of a real believer will cry out to God in prayer.

6) **Selfless Love:** A true believer will put others before himself. Someone who can't love others is not a Christian. If a person finds it hard to love themselves, it will become even more difficult to love others. The best example of selfless love is Christ, for Matthew 20:28 tells us, "Just as the Son of Man did not come to be served, but to serve, and to give his life as a ransom for many."

7) **Separation from the World:** John 17:15-18 says, "If anyone loves the world, the love of the Father is not in him." Though we have to live *in* the world, we do not have to be *of* the world. We should be focused on heavenly, eternal things, not the material things of this world.

8) **Spiritual Growth:** We don't need to get hung up on how we grow. We just need to know that the spiritual life is within us and it will grow, as we develop a deeper trust and dependence on God.

9) **Obedient Living:** By living out God's Word and allowing ourselves to become an extension of Him, we will enjoy living with an abundant life, while embracing the saving faith of Christ.

We must understand that living a life of performance standards will only lead to frustration and defeat. We are not justified because of what we do. Justification is done on the part of God. We cannot declare ourselves "not guilty." There is nothing you can do to keep from being guilty of the sins you've committed, other than accept the free gift of salvation in faith. When this act occurs, we are flooded with grace. Why? Because we receive something that we cannot earn, nor that we deserve from a holy God.

CHAPTER 14
ABRAHAM: JUSTIFIED BY FAITH
Romans 4:1-12

*"What does the Scripture say? 'Abraham believed God, and it was
credited to him as righteousness.' Now when a man works, his
wages are not credited to him as a gift, but as an obligation.
However, to the man who does not work but trusts God who
justifies the wicked, his faith is credited as righteousness."*
- Romans 4:3-5

Paul was aware that the Romans knew a lot about Jewish
history. So, in this section of his letter, he points them to the
example of Abraham, the father of the Jewish/Christian faith. Jews
were proud to be called children of Abraham, so Paul uses
Abraham as an example of someone saved by faith. Here's the
question: Did Abraham's good works and acts of obedience save
him or was he saved by his faith? If there's any part of the Bible
that gets twisted and distorted it's the doctrine of salvation. If
Satan can cause us to be confused in this one part of the Bible, he
succeeds in keeping us under his control. Every other religion in
the world is developed around some form of salvation by works. In
other words, the concept is that you must do something to pay back
God for your salvation. This totally erodes the biblical doctrine of
salvation.

Paul devotes the entire fourth chapter of Romans to
Abraham in order to illustrate the point that man can only become
right with God by **faith** in response to His grace, never by **works**.
Paul uses Abraham for a reason: He was human, but he was the
most respected person of all Jews. Up to this point Paul has simply
outlined the theological truths of salvation. By using Abraham, he
gives us a live, flesh-and-blood illustration. Abraham was a
biblical model of genuine faith for the Jews. Most Jews believed
that he was connected to God because of his righteous character.

They saw him as the most faultless man. In a way, they saw him as a human god. Therefore, when Paul teaches that Abraham's works, righteousness, and obedience did not justify him, he demolishes the foundations of the entire Jewish belief system. If keeping the Law could not make Abraham righteous, then what hope is there for them? However, it follows that, if Abraham was declared "not guilty" solely based on his faith in God, then everyone else must be saved in the same way. Paul reverses course: He does a flea flicker, a football play that usually catches the other team off guard. He catches the Jews off guard with his argument.

Verses 1-2: *"What then shall we say that Abraham, our forefather, discovered in this matter? If, in fact, Abraham was justified by works, he had something to boast about – but not before God."* Here's what Paul is saying: Because we agree that Abraham is the perfect example of a man justified (declared "not guilty") in God's sight, why don't we look at him carefully in order to determine the basis of his salvation? Paul shows us that Scripture teaches Abraham was saved by his faith alone. "According to his flesh" refers to physical lineage. Also, it refers to human effort. If we could be declared "not guilty" before God because of our efforts, then we would have grounds for boasting for all the "good" things we do. But Paul points out that we cannot do anything to boast about before God. <u>This also drives home the point that no Christian ever needs to feel better than someone else because our boasting should not be about ourselves, but always about God.</u>

Verses 3-5: *"What does the Scripture say? 'Abraham believed God, and it was credited to him as righteousness.' Now when a man works, his wages are not credited to him as a gift, but as an obligation. However, to the man who does not work but trusts God who justifies the wicked, his faith is credited as righteousness."* – "Abraham believed God, and it was credited to him as righteousness." Justification never means to make a person righteous. It only means that, when we have faith in God, we are declared "not guilty" and He treats us as if we are righteous. The principle of "justification by faith" rests on the foundation that God imputes righteousness to the ungodly as a free gift. We cannot earn salvation. Rather, it is freely given when we put our trust and faith in the substitutionary death atonement of Jesus Christ. We know that faith means simply believing that God is who He says He is and can do what He says He can do. Our faith allows us to simply accept God's free gift of eternal life.

Verses 6-8: *"David says the same thing when he speaks of the blessedness of the man to whom God credits righteousness apart from works: 'Blessed are they whose transgressions are forgiven, whose sins are covered. Blessed is the man whose sin the Lord will never count against him.'"* What can we do to get rid of guilt? Forgiveness removes guilt and joy is found when we:

1) Confess our sins before God.

2) Ask God for forgiveness.

3) Let go of the guilt and trust God that He has forgiven us.

4) Forgiveness sets us free. Sins confessed are sins forgiven.

1 John 1:9 says, "If we confess our sins, He is faithful and just and will forgive us our sins and purify us from all unrighteousness."

CHAPTER 15
RIGHTEOUSNESS COMES BY FAITH
Romans 4:13-17

"It was not through Law that Abraham and his offspring received the promise that he would be heir of the world, but through the righteousness that comes by faith." - Romans 4:13

In the last chapter we talked about what Paul tells us in Romans 4:3, "Abraham believed the Lord, and He credited it to him as righteousness." Let's turn to Galatians 3:2: "I would like to learn just one thing from you: Did you receive the Spirit by observing the Law, or by believing what you heard?" What he's asking is: Do we receive God's Spirit in our life because we do good deeds, go to church, read our Sunday School lessons, help old ladies cross the street, and sing in the choir? Think about it. Will any of those things cause us to receive the Spirit of God in our life? No. But what if we truly believe in God? That's exactly what Abraham did. He simply believed in God, His love, His power, His awesomeness, His grace, and His mercy. We receive God's Spirit when we believe in Christ. His spirit is our means to be connected with God. His Spirit guides us and directs us as we live each day.

Here in Galatians, **Paul is trying to tell us that human effort has nothing to do with salvation.** In the church of Galatia, many of the church members were individuals who witnessed a life-changing experience in their own lives. They received the Holy Spirit and knew that they did nothing but simply believe God in Christ and they were now changed people. But they had taken a step backward when they insisted on following the Jewish laws. Many times new believers do the same thing. They fall into a trap of tradition. The type of music, worship style, Lord's Supper, and programs sometimes become the object of worship instead of simply placing our total focus on Christ. I like what Rick Warren said in the opening statement of his book, *The Purpose Driven*

Life: "It's not about me, it's about God." That one statement radically changed my view of my faith-walk with the Lord. It drove me to a deeper understanding of discovering who I am in Christ.

We must understand the very important principle that spiritual growth occurs when we allow Christ to take over our lives. As we let Christ come into us, He compels a transformation process. **The hardest principle to understand is that it's not how hard we work; it's how much we allow Him to work through us.** In today's world, it's easy for us to get caught up in trying to find security in our accomplishments. We feel like there must be more to it than this. To us, simply believing and having faith alone in Christ seems too easy. The key to a life developed in Christ is believing by faith and never letting anything take the place of walking with Him. The only way we can live for God is through the power of the Holy Spirit.

Our human tendency is to do those things which seem to be exciting. Sometimes we take the position that if something isn't exciting there's something wrong with us spiritually. The other day I was hitting golf balls while my instructor watched, giving me detailed tips. I hit several really good shots, but then on the next shot I pushed the ball about 30 yards right of my target. I looked up and asked my instructor, "What caused that?" He said, "Let's stop for a moment. I want to talk to you about something very important. If you hit one bad shot, don't ask, 'What am I doing wrong?' I want you to change your thinking to, 'Let's do what I've been doing to hit it right.' In other words, I want you to keep doing the things I'm teaching you and if you mess up, just go back to what's right. Don't focus on what's wrong." Sometimes in our spiritual life we do the same thing. Most of the time we focus on all our baggage when Christ wants us to stay focused on Him. Peter gives us a vivid illustration of this principle of always focusing on Christ when he got out of the boat and walked on the water. Why did he sink? He took his eyes off of Christ.

Let's read verses 13-15: *"It was not through Law that Abraham and his offspring received the promise that he would be heir of the world, but through the righteousness that comes by faith. For if those who live by Law are heirs, faith has no value and the promise is worthless, because Law brings wrath. And where there is no Law there is no transgression. "* Paul is saying that a Christian becomes born again, not based on the Law but through faith in Christ. Let's turn to Genesis for a moment. Abraham was given a covenant from God when he was 75 years old (Genesis 12:1-4). Abraham was declared righteous (Genesis 15:6). Circumcision was introduced when he was 99 years old (Genesis 17:1-14). Now here's the point: Abraham had faith in God for 24 years before he was circumcised. Why? The message is that everyone in the world can have the opportunity to be put right with God by faith alone, not because they follow a bunch of rituals. Ceremonies and rituals are reminders of our faith. They encourage and uplift us spiritually, but they do not give us any special merit before God. Is there anything in your life you have put before God?

Following traditions is an outward sign of our inward belief of His saving power. Biblical traditions are good. God gave us tradition for the sole purpose of keeping a sharp focus on Him. Oftentimes we substitute the act of the tradition for Him. When this occurs, we have put the things God created above the Creator. The focus of our faith should always remain on Christ and His saving actions, not on our saving actions. Some churches promote people more than they do Christ. Mostly they promote what people do. There's nothing wrong with rewarding people for their efforts but the focus of our faith needs to be in Christ. **We are saved by faith and by the grace of the living God in Christ.** Loving God does not save us, doing good does not save us, even doing good plus faith does not save us. It's faith alone. Having faith and believing in Christ and trusting Him to forgive our sins is all that's needed.

So, if all this is true, why even have the Law? What is the purpose of the Law? Let's go to Galatians 3:24: "So the Law was put in charge to lead us to Christ that we might be justified by faith." The Law shows us how bad we are without Christ. We cannot live up to the Law; therefore, the Law is a clear indication that we need help. If there is no way we can live up to the Law and if we are going to be condemned to hell if we ever miss the mark, what do we do? This is where we let God be God. What do I mean by this?

When we let God be God we are allowing Him to do for us what we cannot do for ourselves. We cannot live up to the Law ourselves so we are helpless without God. We cannot save ourselves, but that's where His Son, Jesus Christ, comes into the picture. At some point, we realize the harder we work, the further behind we get without God's help. Work follows effort. In this picture of God and us, who does the work? God does. Think about this illustration: The interstate highway is full of trucks pulling trailers. In this analogy, who's the truck and who's the trailer? God is the truck. Now why is He the truck? He is the truck because He is pulling us. Who is the trailer? We are the trailer because we are following Him. Here's my next question: How far can we go with the trailer leading the truck? We can go nowhere. How many trucks have you seen getting pulled by a trailer? You have not seen any. Why? You saw none because it's impossible. The fundamental principle of Christianity is to realize that God is the truck and our job is to go exactly where He wants us to go. What would happen if the trailer tried to drive the truck? There would be a huge wreck.

Many Christians never understand this principle and, as a result, are trying to pull the truck with the trailer, leaving their lives in a total wreck. If you've been doing it backwards it's time to stop and let Christ take over and become the Lord of your life.

CHAPTER 16
STAY FOCUSED ON GOD
Romans 4:18-25

"Yet he did not waver through unbelief regarding the promise of God, but was strengthened in his faith and gave glory to God."
- Romans 4:20

This chapter will conclude Romans 4, which is primarily focused on Abraham's faith. If we look closely at these last few verses, we will find that Paul's illustration of Abraham is the main example in the Old Testament of saving faith. Paul gives us a clear picture that it requires man's faith and God's grace before salvation is complete. Ephesians 2:8-10a says, "For by grace you have been saved through faith and not of yourselves. It is a gift of God, not as a result of works, that no one should boast. For we are His workmanship."

Abraham's original name was Abram, which means "father of many" (Genesis 12:1-2). God called Abram into a covenant and told him that his descendants would be as many as the stars in the heavens. Now let's stop and think about this for a moment. He was 75 years old when God told him this. Abram was a rather wealthy man who was married to a woman named Sarah. They could not have children, which, in that day, was looked at almost like a curse. So, when God told Abram he would have many descendants he did not understand. **Many people made fun of Abram, a man whose name indicated a multitude of descendants, yet he did not even have one child as proof of his name, not to mention that he was growing old.**

Like Abraham, every person is facing a challenge in their life today that is larger than them. Some have more bills than money, broken relationships, or health issues - things that seem so huge they cannot be fixed.

Understand this: **God's will for us will always be larger than we think and larger than we can accomplish.** Do you know why that is? Because He wants us to be in a position where we must put our absolute trust and faith in Him, for His glory instead of ours. If we like to see our name in lights and want everyone to know we're special, we're not ready to experience a new life in Christ. **God will have to humble us and break us to the point that we understand that we are nothing and He is everything.** At that point, He can put us back together to be used by Him.

Paul continues in the last few verses of this lesson by showing us that faith also comes by divine power, not human effort. Turn to Genesis 17:18-19: "And Abraham said to God, 'If only Ishmael might live under your blessing!' Then God said, 'Yes, but your wife Sarah will bear you a son, and you will call him Isaac. I will establish my covenant with him as an everlasting covenant for his descendants after him.'" When they reached old age, Abraham and Sarah had tried to take the matter of having a child into their own hands by having Ishmael through Hagar. But God knew what he was doing and Sarah miraculously became pregnant with Isaac. God used Isaac as proof of his divine power and blessed Abraham. **Outside of God's will, human efforts will create destruction. God's promises can only be fulfilled by God's power.** No matter how clever or wise you think you are, following God's plan always leads to a life of peace and freedom in the Lord.

Paul outlines **seven** key characteristics of Abraham's God-given faith:

1) **He believed in hope.** Hope and faith are related but not the same. Hope is the desire for something that might be true or might happen. Faith is the firm confidence that it is true and will happen. The object of Abraham's faith was God. He hoped when there was no reason to hope. He believed it would happen.

2) **Abraham believed God without becoming weak in his faith.** Abraham truly trusted God. Do you find yourself relying on your own efforts instead of placing all your trust in God, regardless of your circumstances?

3) **His faith kept him from becoming discouraged.** His power to have a child was gone. God took away the power of human effort. Let me ask you a question: What has God taken away so that you will be totally dependent on Him? Are you willing to place all your trust in the living Christ?

4) **He believed even when Sarah's womb was dead.** When things seem hopeless we often lose faith. Why? Because we see it as failure. God sees it as opportunity to show His glory and reveal His power.

5) **When things were impossible, Abraham stood strong in faith.** It's easy to trust God when things are going great, but when we face the impossible the human effort element kicks in and says, "Let me do it. I will get it done." When God tested Abraham, guess what happened? He grew strong in faith (James 1:2-4). A great theologian once wrote, "Godly faith is not full understanding, but full trust."

6) **Godly faith glorifies God.** The One who gives faith gets the credit. We must be careful to never steal the glory of God. It's so easy to feel that you deserve credit, but all credit belongs to God.

7) **God's promise is certain and His power is sufficient.** The promises of God will not return void. The power of God is more than enough. God's provision will always be sufficient to accomplish the task He has called you to do.

CHAPTER 17
PEACE & JOY
Romans 5:1-5

"And hope does not disappoint us, because God has poured out his love into our hearts by the Holy Spirit, whom he has given us."
- Romans 5:5

When Jesus walked the earth, He was Emmanuel, "God with us" (Matthew 1:23). Now, Christ, or the hope of glory, is inside each and every believer. Christ works in and through all things in the believer's life to grow them to be more like Him in every circumstance, to develop perseverance and character. Paul tells us that, "Character produces hope and such hope never disappoints" (Romans 5:5a). Through his letter, Paul teaches the Romans that hope is based on God's reliable attributes and that it grows as they meditate on God's promises. Most people spend more time talking, thinking, and reading about their *problems* rather than the *promises* of God.

Christian hope, simply defined, is a positive attitude toward the future because we place our hope in the crucified, risen, and soon-to-return Jesus who is our Lord and Savior. Some hopes are based on nothing more than a wish for greener pastures. Many people buy lottery or raffle tickets. Their "hope" of winning becomes their noose for hanging. Hope just for hope's sake is not always healthy or productive - we have to place our hope in the right thing. To the Christian, hope is central to our faith. And, as Christians, we live with a hope that is secured by no one less than God himself and His Son, Jesus Christ.

Verses 1-2: *"Therefore, since we have been justified through faith, we have peace with God through our Lord Jesus Christ, through whom we have gained access by faith into this* *grace in which we now stand. And we rejoice in the **hope** of the glory of God.* " – "We rejoice in the hope of the glory of God."

Christ lives in each and every believer as their hope for glory. These first two verses explain that, as Christians, we have been made right with God. This is the simple meaning of the phrase "justified by faith," that we have looked at in previous chapters. Our belief and trust in Jesus Christ as Lord and Savior brings peace between God and us. Being in this spiritual state of peace has many benefits, not the least of which is that we can look forward to the future with confident expectation that God will keep His promise to take us to live with Him for eternity. Our "hope of the glory of God" is in knowing that God will be faithful to us, and that no matter what may happen in the present, our future is secure. Christ works in and through all things in the believer's life to build our character to be more like Him in every circumstance.

Verses 3-4: *"Not only so, but we also rejoice in our sufferings, because we know that suffering produces perseverance; perseverance, character; and character, **hope**."* Now, Paul uses "hope" at the end of a chain of events that begins with suffering.

Paul teaches the Romans that their hope grows out of godly character, which will help them to adapt and grow in any situation. The great truth about hope in God is that it is not diminished by circumstances, criticisms, or misfortunes. Hopeful people in desperate times are given a greater opportunity to share their testimony of confidence in Christ. It is a call to accept the reality of suffering in our lives, trusting that God will help us through it. Nothing great has ever been accomplished when a deep sense of hope did not occur. Again, Christ works in and through all things in the believer's life to build their character to be more like Christ in every circumstance.

Verse 5: *"And **hope** does not disappoint us, because God has poured out his love into our hearts by the Holy Spirit, whom he has given us."* The Holy Spirit in our lives is like a deposit made by God - a guarantee - that one day all He has promised and much, much more will happen. Hope is built on the love of God in our lives. Psalm 33:18 says, "But the eyes of the Lord are on those who fear Him, on those whose hope is in His unfailing love." Hope is a powerful motivation of life. Hope in ourselves, hope in materialism, and hope in relationships are very fragile at best. Our hope can be firmly established in the almighty, Lord Jesus. **This is the only true hope that exists for all of mankind.**

A Christian's hope also stands on the undeniable existence and redemptive work of Jesus Christ. 1 Thessalonians 1:3 says, "We continually remember before our God and Father your work produced by faith, your labor prompted by love, and your endurance inspired by hope in our Lord Jesus Christ." The end of this section in Romans declares that our hope is also built on the presence of the Holy Spirit in our lives. As followers of Christ, we are anchored to nothing less than Christ Himself, so we should, as His children, live lives that show this hope to be alive and real.

When things of calamity occur in the world, Christians should remain calm and always remember the promises of God. Hope steadies our hearts in the present and prepares us for the future. It also leads us to do things in the power of the Holy Spirit, which would be "hopeless" without Him.

CHAPTER 18
THE UNCONDITIONAL LOVE OF CHRIST
Romans 5:6-11

"But God demonstrates his own love for us in this: While we were still sinners, Christ died for us." - Romans 5:8

In the last chapter we went through the first five verses of Romans 5. Before moving on, I'd like to take a few minutes to review. To understand the next four chapters, it helps to keep in mind the two-sided reality of the Christian life. On one hand, we are complete in Christ – our acceptance with Him is secure – because of the exchange of Jesus' righteousness. On the other hand, we are striving to grow in Christ – becoming more like Him. We have both the status of kings and the duties of slaves. We feel both the presence of Christ and the pressure of sin. Not only do we have the joy and the peace that comes from knowing Christ as our Savior, but we also face daily problems that cause us to grow in faith.

We must understand both sides of the Christian life. If we do, we will not get discouraged as trials come upon us. Instead, we will learn how to depend on the power available to us by way of the Holy Spirit. Our relationship with God begins with faith – the firm belief that God is real and alive and wants to live in and through our lives. Only then can hope grow in us as we discover the character of God, His promises, and His power. **Hope gives us a guarantee of the future.** Next is love. We can do nothing, the Bible teaches us, without love. 1 Corinthians 13:13 tells us, "And now these three remain: faith, hope and love. But the greatest of these is love." **God's love fills us and gives us the ability to love others.** The depth of your love for others reflects the depth of your love for God. You cannot truly love God without also loving other people. The entire focus of the Bible is based on love. It is the deep, rich love that comes from God that grows us into who He wants us to be.

Verse 3: *"Not only so but we also rejoice in our sufferings, because we know that suffering produces perseverance."* Rejoice in your sufferings. Do you currently have any problems in your life? **Problems are good.** Why? Because the bigger the problem, the more pain we have and the more we depend on the Lord. **As our trust deepens, our character is shaped and we become less confident in ourselves and more dependent on God about the future.**

Now on to verse 6: *"You see, at just the right time, when we were still powerless, Christ died for the ungodly."* We are weak and powerless. We are sinners without God. We cannot do anything to save ourselves, so God sent His only Son to rescue us. It's not your strength God needs it's your weakness.

Verse 8: *"But God demonstrates his own love for us in this: While we were still sinners, Christ died for us."* – "While we were still sinners." What does this mean? While we were utterly helpless before God, totally undeserving of His love, and unworthy of His grace. We are all powerless to escape sin, powerless to escape death, powerless to resist Satan, and powerless to have a relationship with God on our own in any way. Therefore, God amazingly devoted His ultimate unconditional love to us by sending His Son to die on our behalf. He demonstrated the perfect love. The kind of love you and I have for one another most often is totally different. Humans primarily reciprocate love – we love those who love us. It's easy to love someone who loves you back, but to love someone who hates you is a love that only comes from the living Christ. In other words, we put conditions on our love. God's love is totally unconditional while we were still sinners.

Verse 10: *"For if, when we were God's enemies, we were reconciled to Him through the death of his Son, how much more, having been reconciled, shall we be saved through his life!"* God delivers us not only from our initial sin as we become born again, but also from our present sins and struggles. God's grace is sufficient when we fully become His children. **All blessings come from Christ.** We clearly see this in the book of Romans:

1) Peace comes from God. (v. 1)

2) Grace and the hope of glory. (v. 2)

3) God's love poured into our hearts by His Spirit. (vv. 3-4)

4) Delivered from sin by the atonement of His death. (vv. 5-7)

5) Deliverance from His wrath. (v. 8)

6) Reconciliation with God. (v. 9)

7) Preservation during this life. (v. 10)

The love that led Christ to die for all of us sinners is the same love that allows the Holy Spirit to live in us and guide us every day. The power that raised Jesus from the dead is the same power that saves us from ourselves and is available for daily living. **God is waiting on us to call on Him for the power of daily living and the support of His love.**

Verse 11: *"Not only is this so, but we also rejoice in God through our Lord Jesus Christ, through whom we have now received reconciliation."* We rejoice because God did for us what we could not do for ourselves. He took our punishment on the cross. This is unconditional love. Since Christ did this for us, we are able to have a direct connection with God through Christ. Because we can best identify with something we can see, feel, touch, and experience, Christ came to earth as both 100% God and 100% human. Christ is the perfect Savior, the perfect sacrifice, the perfect redeemer, the perfect friend. Because of Christ, we are set free from the burdens of our sin and the burdens of the world. He is the perfect example to follow in order to lead a complete life on earth and forever.

If God demonstrated His love while we were a bunch of good-for-nothings, what does that tell us about our duties as Christians? Once we have Christ, we are called to demonstrate the love of God for others regardless of what they say or do to us. God will ultimately put every one of us in a position to love those who hate us. It's a test that measures our maturity in Christ. It takes a mature Christian to pass the test. **Love your worst enemy.** Pastors, love the biggest troublemaker in your congregation as much as the largest giver. **We must allow God's Holy Spirit to teach us how to love the people we hate.** We must let God's Holy Spirit give us the power to overcome obstacles in our lives.

CHAPTER 19
A LIFE IN CHRIST
Romans 5:12-17

"For if, by the trespass of the one man, death reigned through that one man, how much more will those who receive God's abundant provision of grace and of the gift of righteousness reign in life through the one man, Jesus Christ."- Romans 5:17

Have you ever stopped to think how one man could influence all of mankind? How could the sin of one man cause the world to be sinners (Genesis 2:15-17)? Adam and Eve were the first two people God created. They were made in His image. In other words, they were designed and constructed differently than any other creature. Humans have souls. No other creature God created has a soul. When Adam and Eve disobeyed God their disobedience formed a disease called sin. Sin separated Adam and Eve from God. Eve was the first person to sin, but Paul places the blame ultimately on Adam for the sins of mankind. Why? God gave Adam the direct command not to eat from the tree and he had leadership over Eve. He should have insisted on their mutual obedience. You see, herein lie some of the fundamental principles of the Christian life:

1) **All men have a free will.** Adam had the power of choice and because of his choice to disobey God the consequence was sin, resulting in punishment.

2) **The choices we make determine our future.** In addition, there is an order to all the madness. God's order is God, Christ, and man. This is the order. Adam is ultimately responsible even though Eve first committed the sin. Why? Because of the order of God.

Verse 12: *"Therefore, just as sin entered the world through one man, and death through sin, and in this way death came to all men, because all sinned."* – "Sin entered the world through [Adam]." Notice Paul did not say sin originated with Adam, because it was actually brought into the world by Satan. Satan influenced Adam and infected him with the sin disease. The death of mankind is a result of sin. We don't just become sinners. We are sinners because of our nature. Sin equals death and spiritual death is simply separation from God. This concept of sin and righteousness is powerful. What was the purpose of the Law? To help people see their sin and to point them to Christ. <u>Sin is a deep division between who we are and who we were created to be.</u> The Law gives us the context of our sins, but does not give us a remedy to satisfy our sin other than death. So, in effect, the Law gives us the rules to show us how sinful we are, which points us directly to the Savior Christ. It's by God's grace that we are made whole through His only Son.

Verses 13-14: *"For before the Law was given, sin was in the world. But sin is not taken into account when there is no Law. Nevertheless, death reigned from the time of Adam to the time of Moses, even over those who did not sin by breaking a command, as did Adam, who was a pattern of the one to come."* Death is universal. We cannot escape death. Even when the Law did not exist, there was still death "from the time of Adam."

Verse 15: *"But the gift is not like the trespass. For if the many died by the trespass of one man, how much more did God's grace and the gift that came by the grace of the one man, Jesus Christ, overflow to the many!"* Death came through one man, Adam. Eternal life comes through one man, Christ. We are all born into the physical family of Adam and, because of sin, we all face eternal death. Every person in the world has inherited the sinful nature; our souls are separated from God, producing a spiritual death. However, God offers all mankind a way to trade death for life, a way to trade judgment for forgiveness, and a way to exchange our sins for the righteousness of Christ. Just like we were born into the family of Adam, we have the opportunity to choose a new-born life into the family of God through Christ. Christ's family tree starts with forgiveness and leads to life eternal. If we choose to do nothing, we choose death through Adam; but if we come to God in faith, we have a new life in Christ. So, here's the question: **What family do you want to belong to?**

Verse 17: *"For if, by the trespass of the one man, death reigned through that one man, how much more will those who receive God's abundant provision of grace and of the gift of righteousness reign in life through the one man, Jesus Christ."* This is another great principle of the Christian life. 2 Peter 3:18 commands us to, "Grow in the grace and knowledge of our Lord and Savior Jesus Christ." The principle is it's not about a set of rules and regulations or lists of do's and don'ts. Rules don't transform; only a defined relationship with Christ changes who we are. When we operate around a set of rules, we create habits for a period of time, but rules won't transform us from the inside out. Most of our society wants 3 steps to success, 10 steps to become sober, 8 steps to get off drugs. We cannot reduce our faith in Christ to a set of steps. If we do, we make it mechanical instead of relational.

Philippians 1:6 gives us two wonderful promises:

1) If God starts something in our life, His plan is to finish it. His goal is to transform us into His likeness.

2) Maturity in Christ is not a destination; it's a growth process that will work within us from the moment we receive Christ through the rest of our life.

CHAPTER 20
JUDGEMENT CAN BE TRADED FOR FORGIVENESS
Romans 5:18-21

"Consequently, just as the result of one trespass was condemnation for all men, so also the result of one act of righteousness was justification that brings life for all men."
- Romans 5:18

What was Jesus' sole purpose while here on earth? The fundamental and sole purpose of Jesus' life was to do the will of God. **John 4:34 says, "My food is to do the will of the Father who sent me and to finish His work."** "Food" here means spiritual nourishment, which comes from reading God's Word, praying, and fellowship, but most of all, doing His will. John 5:30b tells us, "For I seek not to please myself but Him who sent me." John 6:38 says, "For I have come down from Heaven not to do my will but to do the will of Him who sent me." Jesus' life was characterized by His perfect obedience to His Heavenly Father. Jesus continuously sought to be led by God, to do His will. Philippians 2:8 says, "He humbled Himself by becoming obedient to the point of death, even death on a cross."

Verse 18: *"Consequently, just as the result of one trespass was condemnation for all men, so also the result of one act of righteousness was justification that brings life for all men."* Paul tells us here that one man brought condemnation for all men. Adam penalized the entire human race because of his disobedience; but, Paul reminds us, one act of **righteousness** in Christ sets us free. What is righteousness? Obeying God. The one act of Jesus obeying God was justification for all of our sins. As we know, justification is being declared "not guilty." If we are willing to recognize our sinful nature, admit we are useless without God, repent, turn from, and forsake our sins, and put our trust and faith in Him, He will empower us to live a true Christ-like life. Paul is expressing in very clear terms the importance of Christ's obedience and willingness to do God's will. We would not be able to be redeemed without the obedience of Christ. In this same way, Jesus provides us with a perfect example of how our lives should be shaped in the obedience of Christ. **Our life goal should be to simply do the will of the Father.** To do the will of God one must be connected to God and be led by the Holy Spirit.

Verse 20: *"The law was added so that the trespass might increase. But where sin increased, grace increased all the more."* As a sinner separated from God, you may sometimes try to work and perform, climbing your way up the ladder to God, only to find when you get up two or three steps, you fall off and become frustrated. Has this ever happened to you? Or perhaps you feel totally overwhelmed at the height of the ladder and you are scared to take the first step because you're afraid of what others might say? Paul tells us that Jesus wants to lift us up on the ladder, taking each step with us as we seek His will, and take us directly to God. It is then that we are set free to obey Him and do His will, out of love, not necessity, and through God's power, not our own.

1 John 2:12-14 says, "I write to you, dear children, because your sins have been forgiven on account of His name. I write to you, fathers, because you have known him who is from the beginning. I write to you, young men, because you have overcome the evil one. I write to you, dear children, because you have known the Father. I write to you, fathers, because you have known him who is from the beginning. I write to you, young men, because you are strong, and the word of God lives in you, and you have overcome the evil one." These verses describe three stages of spiritual development:

1) **Stage 1 – Childhood:** When a believer realizes his sins are forgiven through Christ. He understands forgiveness and salvation in Christ.

2) **Stage 2 – Youth / Being Discipled:** When a believer begins to use and rely on scripture to fight temptations and deceptions of the devil.

3) **Stage 3 – Fatherhood / Discipling Others:** When a believer has been discipled, is mature in his faith, and his goal in life is to follow God's will. He knows that this is accomplished through multiplying himself by teaching others.

Each stage is significant in the growth of our Christian faith. We cannot skip a step in the process. **All of us must be discipled. The ultimate goal of every Christian is to invest your life in the life of someone else.** When we do this, we are living out the Great Commission (Matthew 28:19).

Will you allow someone to disciple you in a matter of faith? Will you disciple someone else? To disciple is to simply invest your life into another person. It's living life with a person who is at Stage 3. It's called "Live in Life." It's not just doing a Bible study; no, it's more than that. It's taking the issues of life and handling those issues through the eyes of Christ.

CHAPTER 21
DIE TO SELF, ALIVE IN CHRIST
Romans 6:1-7

"What shall we say, then? Shall we go on sinning so that grace may increase?"- Romans 6:1

When I was a kid, many times I would do something crazy like spit on the sidewalk, throw trash out the window of the car, play tricks on my brother - all the things I had been taught not to do, but I did them anyway. Why? I did them because I could. Oftentimes, in the spiritual world, we view grace as something that allows us to get by with things. This is called cheap grace. Cheap grace is when we continue to do something out of sync with God's will for our lives, fully knowing what we are doing is sin, but we use grace as our fall back position. We ask forgiveness, but we know we're not going to truly commit ourselves to make the needed adjustments in our lives to get back on course.

Here's the question I have for you: **If forgiveness of sin is guaranteed, do we have the freedom to sin as much as we want?** Paul says, "No." Let me tell you an interesting story. In his early teens, John Newton ran away from England and joined the crew of a slave ship. Several years later he found himself slave to the black wife of a white slave trader in Africa. He was cruelly mistreated. He lived on leftovers from the other slaves' meals and dug up wild yams from the ground at night to survive. After escaping the slavery camp, he lived with a group of natives for a while and eventually managed to become a sea captain.

Newton lived a very ungodly life, but, in 1748 his life was radically changed when he gave his life to Christ. He returned to England and became a selfless and tireless minister of the gospel in London. During this time, he wrote many hymns that are still being sung around the world, including one of the most popular and probably the most sung hymn of all time, "Amazing Grace."

Newton became pastor of a church in England and the churchyard there holds his tombstone with an epitaph that he wrote himself: "John Newton, clerk, once an infidel and libertine, a servant of slaves in Africa was, by the rich mercy of our Lord Jesus Christ, reserved, restored, pardoned and appointed to preach the faith he had long labored to destroy." John Newton came to the point in his life that he saw firsthand the power of God's grace at work in the lives of people. He chose to follow Christ and, therefore, he chose a life of obedience to God. **If you say you believe in God and you continue in rebellion against God, living a life of sin, you may have never truly had a salvation experience.**

Many times we try to use accountability groups or some type of external means to attempt to gain control of our sinful lives. **This is what I call sin under management.** Sin cannot be controlled, it cannot be managed. **It must be killed. The only way to kill sin is to turn it over to Christ.**

Let's turn to 1 Timothy 1:12-13: "I thank Christ Jesus our Lord, who has given me strength, that he considered me faithful, appointing me to his service. Even though I was once a blasphemer and a persecutor and a violent man, I was shown mercy because I acted in ignorance and unbelief." Paul tells us that even though he was a sinner, God still showed him mercy and grace. Go to 1 Corinthians 1:2: "The unrighteous will not inherit the earth. Fornicators, idolaters, adulterers, homosexuals, thieves, those who covet, drunkards, revilers, swindlers, shall not inherit the Kingdom of God." **Sin is the most serious element of a man's life.** In essence, sin reflects who we were; Christ reflects what we can become.

Here's the question: What does your life reflect? Our lives are not made by what we say we are, but from what we actually do. Our actions tell of who we really are.

Verse 1: *"What shall we say, then? Shall we go on sinning so that grace may increase?"* Do we keep sinning because God's grace will cover our sins? Paul goes on to say, "By no means! We died to sin; how can we live in it any longer?" A born again believer is free from the bondage of sin. When we are saved, we start a holy way of life, which is lived by the power of God working in and through our hearts. In an unbeliever, sin infects everything he does because it's his way of life. **But a believer who has a new life yields himself to God's Spirit and has no excuse to continue to habitually sin.** Can a person who says they are saved but lives in continual darkness be a child of God? Many say yes, but Paul says no.

The Western world has watered down the true gospel to a 30-minute microwave gospel presentation. Just because a person raises his hand, says, "Yes" to Christ, goes down front, talks to the pastor, and signs a card, does this get him a ticket to enter heaven? America has streamlined the gospel as merely a conversion experience. In many ways we are failing to live out the gospel. We fail to commit our life to the Lordship of Christ. Many claim Him as Savior, but few claim Him as Lord. **Do you put Him in front of everything in your life? If not, He is not Lord.** It's almost as if we want Him to give us our ticket to heaven, and then just leave us alone. Is Jesus your Lord or is He an insurance policy you hope to use at the end of your life?

We have become independent-minded individuals who have prospered off the blessings of our forefathers who founded this country and intentionally sought after the heart of God. God wants us to be interdependent. When we are independent we become self-reliant and cut ourselves off from people. **Jesus was always connected to people.** Many Christians today are isolated from the real world. They surround themselves with people who look like them, talk like them, and live like them. They are disconnected from the world. Jesus tells us that we are the salt and light of the world (Matthew 5:13-16). **How can we light up a part of the world if we refuse to enter into that part of the world?**

Verse 2: *"By no means! We died to sin. How can we live in it any longer?"* How can we die to one life and still live for another? We can't. When we die, what happens – we're put into a coffin and buried. **Paul is telling us to bury our old self**. If the old self is not yet buried, we've never been saved. A spiritual life cannot co-exist with spiritual death. 1 John 3:9 says, "No one who is born of God practices sin" because His seed abides in him and he cannot repeatedly sin because he is born of God. When we truly have the resurrected Christ in our life, sin is overcome by the power of Christ. When we really get saved, we are redeemed. God not only declares us righteous, but he also begins to develop Christ's righteousness in us.

Salvation is not merely a transaction; it's a miracle of transformation. Our salvation will never be perfected because the Christian life is a process "until the day of Christ Jesus." Philippians 1:6 says, "Being confident of this, that he who began a good work in you will carry it on to completion until the day of Christ Jesus." **When Christ comes into our lives, our old self becomes a corpse – it has no life.** So, the **old self** has no potential because he is totally sinful and cannot please God; but the **new self**, the man who has come to Christ in faith, realizing he is hopeless without Christ, has been put right with God. He is pleasing to God because of Christ and his new nature is entirely godly and righteous. The new man is spiritually alive and the holiness of God is at work in his life. We cannot have a divine life without divine living. **Salvation is not only a transaction; it's a transformation.**

Verse 3: *"Don't you know that all of us who were baptized into Christ Jesus were baptized into His death?"* Here, Paul outlines three key principles as they relate to our relationship with Christ:

1) **All true Christians have been baptized into Christ Jesus.** Paul is not talking about being baptized with water. Water baptism is a symbol or outward expression of being immersed into Christ. Some believe that we must be immersed into water to be saved. That's not true. What is true is that salvation is by grace through faith in Christ. Paul is speaking metaphorically of a spiritual immersion of believers into Christ through the Holy Spirit. Galatians 3:27 says, **"For all of you**

who were baptized into Christ have clothed yourselves with Christ." In Roman society a young boy coming of age would lay down the robe of childhood and put on a new toga. This new robe symbolized his move into adulthood, which gave him the rights and responsibilities of Roman citizenship. Similarly, when we become a Christian, we lay aside our old ways, are immersed into Christ, and put on the new clothes of righteousness. We are totally surrounded by and unified with Christ when we have died to our old ways and are clothed with Christ.

2) **All Christians are identified with Christ in His death and resurrection.** This principle is an extension of the first principle. How are we baptized in His death? **For us to live with Christ, we first must die.** We can't be part of a new life in Christ until our old life has been part of His death. Before we can be counted righteous, we must be declared "not guilty." Upon being declared "not guilty," we become holy, not because of our holiness, but because of the holiness of Christ in us. Show me a man who lives for the Lord and I will show you a man who has died to himself and was buried with Christ and raised with Christ in a new life. Verse 4 says, *"We were therefore buried with him through baptism into death in order that, just as Christ was raised from the dead through the glory of the Father, we too may live a new life."* A new life comes from being committed to Christ in His death. **Death in our lives is essential and must occur before we can live a new life in Christ - death to all of our evil desires, cheating, stealing, deceit, nasty thoughts, and addictions** (Colossians 3:12-14). Being aggressive, hostile, loud, arrogant, boastful, proud, argumentative is not included in a new life in Christ. Romans 6:7 tells us we have been set free from our sin.

3) **Christ lives in me**. Until we understand that the old self must be put to death, there cannot be new life in

Christ within us. When we receive a new life, we change – our heart changes, our spirit changes, we have new hope, new strength, and new faith. None of these blessings is associated with our old self. God says get rid of that old self. Bury it. Nail down the lid on it. Move forward in Christ and don't look back on your old life. Too many of us are still dealing with the things that should be dead. We can only experience the realness of Christ when Christ lives in us. Anything unspiritual is not significant in God's eyes. We are all guilty of focusing sometimes on worldly concerns. **When the old self dies, then we can become dependent upon that which is spiritual – Jesus Christ**. Before being saved, we were slaves to sin; but with Christ we have conquered sin. Galatians 2:20 is a great verse to live by: "I have been crucified with Christ, and I no longer live, but Christ lives in me." God considers believers as if they had died with Christ. We are one with Christ in our relationship. Our power to overcome the challenges we have with sin comes from Christ; we alone are not able.

Let's review the three principles of the process of a true Christian's birth:

1) I have been crucified with Christ. My old self died in the same way Christ died for my sins.

2) The old me does not have any life because it has died. Sin cannot control me anymore.

3) Christ lives in me. I am addicted to Christ. We must be so immersed in Christ that we can't live without Him. That's when we can truly say Christ lives in us.

When are you going to let Christ become more than just an insurance policy in your life? I trust you will seek the awesome realness He has for you.

CHAPTER 22
A BELIEVER DOES NOT FEAR DEATH
Romans 6:8-14

"Now if we died with Christ, we believe that we will also live with him."- Romans 6:8

Here's a question for you: Do you fear death? In this chapter, Paul shows us that we must die a spiritual death before we can have spiritual life. In other words, we must die to ourselves before we have a chance at living a new life in Christ. Our biggest obstacle to walking with the Lord is our sinful self. Once we accept our new life, we are transformed into the likeness of Christ. Every person has the disease of sin. Without Christ, we are bound to the old self, our old nature, which ultimately takes control over our lives. **Most people who are out of fellowship with the Lord have a real fear of death.** A Christian who walks with and trusts God does not fear death. Why? A mature Christian understands that death is a natural process for a believer. The Bible teaches us that we are just "passing through" this world. This is a temporary home for Christians. A believer's real home is in heaven for eternity. Forever is the promise we have with God in heaven.

Let's look at verse 8: *"Now if we died with Christ, we believe that we will also live with him."* How do we die with Christ? Just as Christ died on the cross, paying the penalty for our sins, so will our sins die and be forgiven when we put our total trust and faith in the Lord. **When the death of our old nature occurs, a new life begins with our new nature.** Our new nature reflects the character of Christ, which is the same as the character of God. They are one in the same, so to die with Christ is to also live with Christ.

Verse 9: "For we know that since Christ was raised from the dead, He cannot die again; death no longer has mastery over Him." There are three fundamental truths in this verse:

1) **No need to fear death.** The greatest of all events related to the Christian life is Christ rising from the dead. He is alive. He arose on the third day after He was crucified so that we might live. Other religions, like Islam, Buddhism, Hinduism, Hare Krishna, etc., all worship a dead entity that represents their god or plethora of gods. Only one true Savior has ever existed – Jesus Christ. Christ is the only person/God to overcome death and because of His sacrifice, we, as believers, are given the opportunity to overcome death through him. We, therefore, should have no fear of death.

2) **It's time to die to self.** Since Christ died once and arose from the dead, He cannot die again. So, when we die a spiritual death, meaning we have buried the "**old self**," we then allow Christ to live in faith in our "**new self**." In a way, Christ becomes us. To illustrate: it's like adding cherry Kool-Aid to a pitcher of water. When the Kool-Aid penetrates into the molecules of the water, the molecules of the Kool-Aid make a connection with the molecules of the water. Once the Kool-Aid connects with the water, it is almost impossible to separate the two. This is what happens to a person who has Christ in their life. **Christ penetrates every fiber of their soul and the person has a connection with Him that cannot be separated.** Once the "old self" is dead, it's dead. The problem most of us have is that we never fully died. We have allowed a part of us to live because we really don't want to give that part of us up. Here's my question: **What are the things in your life that you have never buried? Until we bury those things and ask Christ to set us free, we will always live an empty life of stress and confusion, a life absent of joy and peace.** Christ is the only true way for us to release the baggage of our old life.

3) **Resurrected in Christ.** When Christ rose from the grave the gates of hell trembled and Satan realized he was doomed forever. God allows Satan to reign over the earth for this time, but Satan knows his days are numbered. **You see, Satan's life means death and Christ's life means life.** Since the tomb could not hold Christ, the grave will not hold us if we are true believers in the Lord.

Verses 10-11: *"The death He died He died to sin once and for all; but the life He lives, He lives to God. In the same way, count yourselves dead to sin but alive to God in Christ Jesus."* Notice here, one death and one life are mentioned. When we allow Christ to control our lives we are mirroring Christ's obedience to God. **We live for Christ. Christ lives for God. The bottom line is that we do not live for ourselves.** This concept is foreign to the world and difficult for new Christians to clearly grasp. It takes the power of the Holy Spirit to transform us into the likeness of Christ.

Verse 12: *"Therefore, do not let sin reign in your mortal body so that you obey its evil desires."* The fact is that we are all sinners and the only way to overcome sin is to develop a deep relationship or spiritual connection with Christ. Those that do not believe they are sinful are naive. They are also self-righteous. A self-righteous person believes they are better than everyone else and that they have it altogether. **You see, sin has the power to control us. We cannot control sin. The only power to overcome sin is in Christ.** No man on earth, by his own will, can defeat sin. Sin will win every time.

Verse 13: *"Do not offer the parts of your body to sin... but rather offer yourselves to God, as those who have been brought from death to life."* God wants us to dedicate our lives to Him. Everything we have belongs to God – our money, our home, our cars, even our families. Jesus was tempted by Satan, but He refused by praying and replying to Satan with God's Word. The only way we can walk the road of joy and peace is to have a direct connection to God, in Christ, through His Word.

Verse 14: *"For sin shall not be your master, because you are not under the law but under grace."* Here Paul is telling Christians that since they have died to themselves and buried their old ways and have been redeemed by the blood of Christ, they have a new life. A new life in Christ equals grace in Christ. You see, in the Old Testament the Pharisees believed they could become righteous by obeying "the Law." As we know, the Law was a set of standards in the Jewish community that was revised over the years and totaled over 700 different rules. However, Jesus said the only way a man could become righteous under the Law is to obey every rule to perfection. This cannot be accomplished; therefore, man under the Law is guilty before God.

Here's the cool part. When Christ died for us, He paid the penalty for our sins and, because of this, when we believe in Jesus Christ, we are deemed "justified" – we are declared "not guilty" before God. When we are justified, we are instantly seen as **"righteous"** in the eyes of God.

Righteous means that we are put right with God. We are righteous, not because of what we have done, but because of what Christ did. God sent His only Son so that we might be justified in faith and made righteous before a Holy God. When we become a believer, we bury our past and take up a new life and we no longer have to live under the Law. We respect the Law, we obey the Law, but we do not have to live a defeated life under the Law. Never being able to be perfect can leave us frustrated. However, since Christ is perfect and lives in us, we no longer have to live under the Law, trying to achieve something we could never do. Christ has already done it for us.

CHAPTER 23
SIN IS POWERFUL
Romans 6:15-18

"You have been set free from sin and have become slaves to righteousness."- Romans 6:18

In this chapter, we are going to talk about sin and righteousness. **Sin is the most devastating power to ever enter the world.** Sin destroys the human soul. It robs us of our power and our potential. Sin is corrosive, poisonous, rebellious, and selfish. Sin makes us weak against satanic control. Sin promises fun but ends in misery. Paul tells us that the natural man is a willing slave to sin. What is sin? How did sin occur in our world? What is the result of sin? Why do people sin? The final question – how do we overcome sin?

We, in our imperfections, cannot overcome sin by way of self. **Sin is stronger than any single person without Christ.** Sin is when we are doing things that are not in line with God's Word. There's no man on the planet that can overcome sin through his own power. What Paul is saying is that when we accept Christ, we are no longer under the Law but under grace. We must understand that the Law was a dead end. The Law could never be lived up to, because to fulfill the Law, man had to live a perfect life; otherwise, he would be declared "guilty."

So there's no way we can get to Christ without God giving us the grace of salvation in Christ. **Paul gives us two options: Obedience to sin or obedience to Christ.** If we choose Christ, we automatically fall under the authority of the grace of Christ. So, Paul says we no longer live under the Law that we could never live up to. Instead, we are under grace. Because of our faith in Christ, we have been declared "not guilty." **All Christians are saved by grace**. Grace not only justifies us, but it also transforms the life that is saved. **A life that gives no evidence of spiritual transformation gives no evidence of salvation.**

Matthew 6:24 says, "No one can serve two masters. Either he will hate the one and love the other, or he will be devoted to the one and despise the other. You cannot serve both God and money." The point is that a person cannot live two opposing lives. **Once we are saved, we can no longer live in two opposite worlds.** Paul says it's time to either be a slave to sin or be a slave to God in Christ, which results in righteousness. When we accept Christ, we commit our life to a life of **slavery to righteousness**. John says in 1 John 3:9, "No one who is born of God practices sin because His seed abides in him." In other words, when we become a believer, God changes the DNA of our spiritual make-up. He saves us and prepares us to become a righteous person. A true believer cannot continue in sin. It becomes so diametrically opposed to his new, holy nature he will refuse to endure sinful living. John 8:34-35 says, "I [Jesus] tell you the truth, everyone who sins is a slave to sin." 2 Peter 2:19-22 tells us, "For a man is a slave to whatever has mastered him." Be strong in the Lord. **Be a slave to Christ and become a runaway slave to sin.**

Verse 17: *"But thanks be to God that, though you used to be slaves to sin, you wholeheartedly obeyed the form of teaching to which you were entrusted."* It's so important for all of us to obey the teaching of God's Word. 2 Timothy 1:13-14 says, "Guard the good deposit entrusted in you and guard it with the help of the Holy Spirit who lives in us." Paul refers to the believers who fully trusted in Christ. Here are a couple of questions: Have you fully trusted Christ? Have you wholeheartedly obeyed God's Word? Will you start today putting your total trust in Him?

Verse 18: *"You have been set free from sin and have become slaves to righteousness."* As Christians, our ultimate goal should be to become slaves to righteousness. Let me give you four things I believe it takes to be a good slave to God's righteousness in Christ:

1) **Humility:** Get rid of pride. Pride is the opposite of humility. Pride destroys. Pride is a consumer of self. Humility is a consumer of God. Let God break you and shape you with His Word. God's Word will cut away all the pride and humbleness will overtake the core of your personhood.

2) **Obedience to the Master:** Evaluate what God would have you do versus what you want to do and be willing to trust God with His plan and give up your selfish desires. Are you willing to give over yourself to the will of God?

3) **Willingness to work hard:** There is no room for laziness in Christians. We must be willing to exercise our faith in obedience and take spiritual risks. When is the last time you took a spiritual risk? The journey of faith requires us to do our part, not out of duty, but out of love for God.

4) **Give credit to the Master:** We must never get in the way of keeping the light of God's glory shining to the world. When we take credit, God's glory cannot flow through us. God must always receive the glory for He is the Master and it is in Him that we accomplish His work. Notice it's all about Him. It's time for some of us to get over ourselves.

A slave has no rights. A slave is on call 24/7. A slave obeys his master. A slave obeys authority. A slave seeks to please the master. A slave does not seek recognition. A slave is totally dependent on the master for all his needs. A slave never takes credit for his work. To be set free in Christ you must become a slave in Christ.

Will you consider allowing Christ to expose you to His righteousness so that you may learn to become a slave to the righteousness of Christ?

CHAPTER 24
A BELIEVER IS NOT A SLAVE TO SIN
Romans 6:19-23

"I put this in human terms because you are weak in your natural selves. Just as you used to offer the parts of your body in slavery to impurity and to ever-increasing wickedness, so now offer them in slavery to righteousness leading to holiness."- Romans 6:19

This chapter opens up the door to a topic that most Christians have difficulty dealing with. For years I had good intentions of exercising while the treadmill sat in the corner of the bedroom with clothes hanging from the side rails. Do you know what the most grueling thing is for us to do? Open the door of self-examination. **Examining ourselves forces us to evaluate the things that are not healthy or good about ourselves.** Sometimes we are blind to negative things about ourselves because Satan uses the tool of manipulation to try to trick and control us. It's always easier to find fault in someone else before we find fault with ourselves. In these verses, Paul tells us that, without Christ as our Master, we, as humans, are controlled by the influences of the world.

There are two types of power – good and pure, which is from God, and evil and corrupt, which is from Satan. Paul says in verse 19a, *"I put this in human terms because you are weak in your natural selves."* Paul wants us to recognize that, without Christ, we are weak. We are unable to cope with the everyday pressures of life. **We are frustrated because there is a real purpose lacking within us.** So he goes on to say in verse 19b, *"So now offer them in slavery to righteousness leading to holiness."* Here Paul gives us a different perspective on how to handle life and overcome our personal circumstances. As Christians we are to **"give everything up to live an obedient life in Christ."** There's a hidden key to this view of life, which is that when we become a believer in Christ, or when we commit our life to follow Him, we receive the power from the Holy Spirit to reject any and all sin that may be in our lives. God's power is sufficient. God's grace is sufficient. There's no need to have a program to overcome your ways. Paul tells us in layman's terms to simply stop what we are doing wrong and become a slave of righteousness. If we are following His teaching on this issue, it will lead to "holy" living. God is pleased when you lead a holy and pure life before Him.

Verse 20: *"When you were slaves to sin, you were free from the control of righteousness."* Paul informs us that before we became believers we could not get out of the trap of the world. The world wants to convince you that what you're doing is okay. We must come to grips with the fact that we will be controlled by an outside force, either controlled by sin, or controlled by the righteousness of God.

Verse 21: *"What benefit did you reap at that time from the things you are now ashamed of? Those things result in death!"* Here Paul hits the rewind button and takes us back to before we believed in Christ. He lets us know that the ways of the world will always end in a spiritual death. **Spiritual death is when we are separated from a relationship with God.** There is only one result from sin and that's death. The result of righteousness is everlasting life.

Verse 22: *"But now that you have been set free from sin and have become slaves to God, the benefit you reap leads to holiness, and the result is eternal life."* In this verse Paul explains how the mechanics of Christianity work:

1) A life in Christ is a life of power over sin – we are **"set free from sin."**

2) We become a slave to God. We are not owners of ourselves. God owns us and we are merely managers of the things we have because everything good comes from God.

3) Holiness comes from living an obedient life.

4) Living for Christ results in living an eternity with Christ in heaven.

Verse 23: *"For the wages of sin is death but the gift of God is eternal life in Jesus Christ our Lord."* Paul shows us that eternal life in Christ is a free gift from God. We are unable to earn a free gift. **A gift is something I give you based on my love for you, not based on your ability to pay me back.** The appropriate response when someone gives you a gift is to accept it with gratitude and grace. Our salvation in Christ is a gift of God, not a reward for something we have done. Ephesians 2:8-9 tells us, "For it is by grace you have been saved, through faith – and this not from yourselves, it is the gift of God – not by works, so that no one can boast." God offers this gift to all people. He shows us mercy, not because of any righteous thing we have done, but because of what He has done through His only Son, Jesus Christ.

The really beautiful part of this picture is that He does not force this gift on us. **We must accept His gift in faith because the gift needs to be activated.** For example, I could give you a gift card from Wal-Mart worth $100, but if you refused to activate the card by using it to make a purchase, the benefit of the card would be lost. In the same way, we have a "card," or a soul, placed within us by God. Before the soul can be activated, we must be willing to receive God's free gift of salvation through faith in Christ. This gift is given to us by the power of the Spirit. **It's God's way of expressing His unconditional love and forgiveness to all people.** It is a means to activate the soul, His redemption for us allows us to be connected to all that God has in store for us on earth and in heaven.

God initiates the gift through the effectual usage of the Holy Spirit. Accepting the gift of salvation is our choice; God does not force salvation on us. He even gives us the strength and the faith we need to come to Him totally helpless, asking for and accepting His gift of salvation. This gift from God is the key that unlocks the door to a life of peace and an eternal life in heaven. If you have never truly activated your soul by accepting God's free gift of salvation, will you consider taking that first step today? Will you allow yourself to commit to a holy way of living, rest peacefully in His grace and love, and be strengthened by His transforming power? The redemptive love of Christ is a clear picture of His true, unconditional love for the entire world.

CHAPTER 25
ONLY JESUS CHRIST CAN SET US FREE
Romans 7:1-6

"So, my brothers, you also died to the law through the body of Christ, that you might belong to another, to him who was raised from the dead, in order that we might bear fruit to God."
- Romans 7:4

In Romans 7:1-6, Paul shows us that the Law is powerless to save the sinner. In the earlier chapters we discussed that we are all condemned before God by the Law and salvation cannot be found by obeying the Law. No matter who we are, only Jesus Christ can set us free. Let me ask you a question: Does the Law apply to me if I'm dead? No. Why? Punishment cannot be imposed against someone who's dead. When we ask Christ into our hearts, guess what happens? **We die. We have died to our old nature, but we become a new creature.** What ruled our old nature? **The Law**. So in effect, we die also to the Law.

Some of us, as Christians, are focused on performance and still have not died to our old way of operating. Our old nature wants everything to be about performance, looking good, and impressing others – in essence, our old nature is about us. Our old nature worries about things all the time. Our old nature will not allow us to totally turn everything over to God and become dependent on Him. Our old nature wants to control its environment. Our old nature wants to be a big shot. Our old nature wants attention and praise. Our old nature feels sorry for itself. Our old nature wants to fight back and to get even. Our problem is not that Christ fails us; our problem is that we often do not trust Christ enough to completely let go of our old self. Before you can be set free, you must let go of focusing on yourself and become reprogrammed to focus on Christ and others.

Do we really understand what it costs to be a follower of Christ? It requires sacrifice. **The first step is to trust Christ, let go, and die to our old nature.** Paul makes the declaration that faith in Christ brings death to the Law and freedom from the Law's penalty. You see, when we allow our old self to die, we are no longer married to the Law. Our first marriage is to Christ, the divine bridegroom of the church. Why are we joined together in a new marriage with Christ? Why do we have a new relationship with Him? What is the real purpose? It is that we might bear fruit. The purpose for our relationship with Christ is to be used of God to multiply the world so that others will have the same marriage or relationship with Christ (Galatians 2:19-20). Spiritual fruit is produced basically in two dimensions:

1) **Attitude**: The Holy Spirit will lead a person to manifest internally the attitudes of love, joy, peace, patience, goodness, faithfulness, self-control (Galatians 5:22-23).

2) **Godly actions**: Our preparation for Christ's second coming. Philippians 1:11 calls us to be "filled with the fruit of righteousness which comes through Jesus Christ."

This is the concept of being set free: If our Christian life is focused around a set of rules, then our old self is still dominant and we will live a frustrated life. But, if we allow God to control our life and let our heart be renewed, we will receive an overflow of God's love that will be reflected in our life. If our self-determination or self will is what's dominant in our life, then that becomes the source of power. If we humbly submit our life to Christ and ask God's Spirit to lead and direct us, then we will be using the power of God. We cannot earn our way to God. Living a performance-based life leads to burn-out. The older I get, the more I realize my freedom is in Christ. My security is in Christ – not in my accomplishments. Many times we lack a self-controlled and a disciplined life, not because we aren't following the rules, but because we don't understand the concept of God's love and grace. When we can allow God's Holy Spirit to turn our eyes away from our own performance and toward Jesus, He frees us to live and serve Him out of love and gratitude. This, my friends, is living **"in the way of the Spirit"** (v. 6). When others do things to hurt you, your natural instinct is to lash out and correct the problem. But

Paul tells us in verse 6 to **"serve in the new way of the Spirit."** To serve in the way of the Spirit means to relinquish all of your selfish desires, all of your anxiety, all of your hatred to the Lordship of Christ and allow Christ to fill your life with His Spirit. We are to be controlled by Christ. A person controlled by Christ is a Spirit filled Christian who produces spiritual fruit. A person who calls himself a Christian, but is in control of himself, is a phony Christian.

CHAPTER 26
OUR STRUGGLE WITH SIN
Romans 7:7-13

"What shall we say, then? Is the law sin? Certainly not! Indeed I would not have known what sin was except through the law. For I would not have known what coveting really was if the law had not said, 'Do not covet.'"- Romans 7:7

In the last chapter we looked in depth at how Jesus Christ sets us free from our old self and our old ways. As prisoners to our old self, after trying to measure up to the Law, we realize we cannot and are always held in the bondage of sin. Before we trust Christ and commit our lives to Him, we are controlled by our old nature. But when we trust Christ to take full control of our lives, we die to the law (vv. 5-6) that we could never live up to. Now we **"serve in the new way of the Spirit"** (v. 6). A man who is lost cannot earn his way to heaven by keeping a set of rules, doing good deeds, and trying to obey the Ten Commandments. He will only become frustrated and discouraged.

Paul tells us to let the Holy Spirit turn our eyes away from our own performance and toward Jesus. The Holy Spirit will free us to serve Him out of love and gratitude. This is what verse 6 is referring to when it talks about living **"in the new way of the Spirit."** In previous chapters, Paul has established that the Law cannot save (Romans 3-5); it cannot sanctify (Romans 6); and it cannot condemn a believer (7:1-6). Now he establishes that the Law can convict both those who follow the Law and those who follow sin (vv. 7-13). Verse 7 poses a very good question. Is the Law sin? In other words, if we must die to the Law, do we have to live by the Law's standards? Does this mean we can live as we please? Paul responds, **"Certainly not!"** The Law is not sinful. **The Law serves as a tool to convict Christians of their sin.** Paul outlines several key points of the importance of the Law to all Christians, but I want to focus this chapter on just one: **The Law reveals sin**.

Verse 7: *"What shall we say, then? Is the law sin? Certainly not! Indeed I would not have known what sin was except through the Law. For I would not have known what coveting really was if the Law had not said, 'Do not covet.'"* The battle with sin is internal. It's a battle in our hearts and our minds. Only the transforming power of the Holy Spirit can take a sinful heart and make it pure and acceptable to God. **The Law's role in a person's transformation is to make us aware of our sin.** It shows us that we need the forgiveness that only God can give and it forces us to either accept or reject the offer of the redemptive work of Christ. The Law shows us that we can never succeed without the strength and power of a genuine relationship with Christ and a spiritual relationship with people.

The problem we have is that we place more faith on external achievements – our goals, our plaques, and our praises of one another. This results in resentment of those we consider successful. Show me one man who has been successful and I'll show you ten guys who talk about him and try to bring him down. We must learn to redefine success. Success cannot be measured by accomplishments or net worth. God defines success by our relationships and obedience to Him. In God's eyes, our relationships with Him and other Christians are what really count.

Can we truly allow God to love us unconditionally without feeling we must earn it by our actions? We must recognize that we do not have to prove to ourselves and others that we are worth being loved. We do not have to gain acceptance from any person. When we try to prove ourselves by being the person everyone else wants us to be we always fail. **God's love is FREE.** Most of us follow the voices of the world. Why do we follow those voices? We want to be accepted. We want to win the love of the world. Following the voices of the world reflects a lack of faith. We must make sure we're following God's plan for our life and no one else's. If we are restful, angry, scared, isolated, lustful, or greedy, we are not being led by God's Spirit and walking with Christ in faith. **Think about this: God loves us so much He refuses to control us. He will never force his love on us.** He has the Holy

Spirit to bring awareness and draw us to Him, but in the end, He allows us to find Him on our own.

Most of us place conditions on our love. Many of us have integrated a performance-based, business approach to life, which has led us to live by performance scorecards. When we do not perform up to the standards we've set, what happens? We get down on ourselves. But here's the deal: We have a choice. Do we accept the things of the world or do we claim the freedom we have as a child of God? Judas betrayed Jesus. Peter denied Jesus. Both were lost children of God. Judas could not take the pressure he put on himself and hung himself. Peter realized his shortcomings and returned with tears. Judas chose death. Peter chose life. My question to you is what will you choose?

Trying to earn God's love is a faulty and unhealthy way to live our life. God loves us where we are. It's okay to pull off the mask and expose our real selves. When we do, we will find real people who are willing to love us in Christ. Those who choose not to love you for who you are may not be the kind of friend you need in your life. Christ wants to forgive us. He wants to love us and restore us. **We cannot restore ourselves.** That's God's job. If we try we will fail and be discouraged. Jesus wants us to simply come to Him as a child. He is pleading for each of us to let God be God. Let Him do for us what we cannot do for ourselves.

Philippians 3:7-9 says, "But whatever was to my profit I now consider loss for the sake of Christ. What is more, I consider everything a loss compared to the surpassing greatness of knowing Christ Jesus my Lord, for whose sake I have lost all things. I consider them rubbish, that I may gain Christ and be found in Him, not having a righteousness of my own that comes from the Law, but that which is through faith in Christ – the righteousness that comes from God and is by faith." Will you give over your struggle with your sin to Christ? Will you trust Him for power to overcome sin? This occurs when we develop a close, intimate walk with Him and discover how awesome His love for us really is.

CHAPTER 27
OUR STRUGGLE WITH SELF
Romans 7:14-25

"We know that the law is spiritual; but I am unspiritual, sold as a slave to sin."- Romans 7:14

For the last several chapters we have dealt with the struggle of sin and how to be set free in Christ. We learned that sin is anything we do that is disobedient to God, falling short of God's standard. **The fundamental reason we have struggles within ourselves is because of sin.** In this chapter, Paul truly exposes himself and tells us how he really feels about his struggle with himself.

Verse 14: *"We know that the Law is spiritual; but I am unspiritual, sold as a slave to sin."* My old self is unspiritual and if I insist on dragging it around with me, I will always struggle in my own strength and fall into the grip of sin's power. **We cannot underestimate the power of sin.** We cannot win the battle of sin by ourselves. None of us, without the Holy Spirit, can go up against sin. God provides every Christian with a unique power, the power of the Holy Spirit. When we fall short it is this divine power that helps us hold it together. Regardless of what your circumstances are in life, always know you have hope in the Lordship of Christ.

Verse 15: *"I do not understand what I do. For what I want to do I do not do, but what I hate I do."* Paul shares three specific, fundamental principles that he learned in trying to deal with his old sinful desires:

1) **Knowledge is not the answer.** He says the more he learned about God the more he saw how bad he was in comparison.

2) **Self-determination is not the answer.** Trying to work our way out of sin will not work. We will always fall short and continue to feel badly about our self.

3) **Good behavior is not the answer.** When we become a Christian, it doesn't mean our life will be free of sin. Becoming like Christ is a life-long process. All of us must rely on the redemptive power of Christ for salvation. We cannot earn it based on our good behavior.

Verse 21: *"So I find this law at work: When I want to do good, evil is right there with me."* Wherever we go, evilness follows us, which is why we must commit ourselves to the Lord daily. **We must die to ourselves each day so that Christ may fully live in us.** Paul shares with us the reality of life. Can you imagine the greatest missionary to ever live struggling with the same issues that you struggle with everyday?

Verse 22: *"For in my inner being I delight in God's law."* **Paul tells us his basic instinct as a Christian is to hunger and thirst for the righteousness of God.** Jesus says in Matthew 5:6, "Blessed are those who hunger and thirst for righteousness because they will be filled." Paul says in 2 Corinthians 4:16, "Though the outer man is decaying, our inner man (spiritual) is being renewed day by day." He also says in Ephesians 3:16 that we can "be strengthened with the power through His Spirit in the inner man."

The more we grow in Christ, the more we hate sin and the more we love humbling ourselves in the righteousness of Christ. As we mature in Christ, we crave a deeper relationship with Him that leads us to serve others without expecting anything in return. Sin is so powerful even a saved person often hangs on to his old self and struggles with his inner self to follow God's will. Without Christ, sin is stronger than we are. Because of our salvation in Christ, there is no reason to try to overcome sin on our own. Christ has conquered sin and we are set free by His power.

Verse 23: *"But I see another law at work in the members of my body, waging war against the law of my mind and making me a prisoner of the law of sin at work within my members."* Here Paul talks about the Law at work in us – the sin that still exists in us that we have not completely given up on. What sin in your life is still lingering around? Paul had this inner struggle and it was real, just as every person has an inner struggle. What's yours? Whatever you are struggling with, here's something you need to know about it:

1) **It's bigger than you are.**

2) **It controls more of you than you realize.**

3) **There's only one way to overcome your struggle –** give it to God every day in prayer. Ask Him to give you strength and set you free.

Do you need a lift? Do you need a confirmation from God about something? God will help you overcome your struggles. Let the reality of Christ's power lift you up to real victory over sin.

Begin to live life from victory not to victory. To live life to victory you are constantly trying to live up to a set of performance driven expectations. To live life from victory means you understand that the victory has already been won in Christ. Knowing the end of the story should give you confidence that Christ understands and will always be with you regardless of the circumstances.

CHAPTER 28

LIFE THROUGH THE SPIRIT
Romans 8:1-8

"Therefore, there is now no condemnation for those who are in Christ Jesus, because through Christ Jesus the law of the Spirit of life set me free from the law of sin and death."- Romans 8:1-2

In our society we have a system of justice. When a person fails to comply with a specific law, a system of justice is used to equal out the offense. **In the spiritual world there is also a justice system.** God's system requires us to either live a perfect life under the Law, which cannot be accomplished, or accept His free gift of salvation and be set free from the Law of sin and death. In chapter 8 of Romans, Paul's asserts that, as believers, those who have a new life in Christ, will not face the punishment they deserve as sinners. If a man is convicted of murder, facing death row, and the judge says there is "no condemnation" found in this man, what does that mean? **Not guilty. Let him go free.**

Verse 1: *"Therefore, there is now no condemnation for those who are in Christ Jesus"* The issue we face is that every human being around the world is on death row. Every person is guilty of sin and, because of that, every person is heading toward an eternal death. God created our soul to live for eternity. Without Christ we are condemned to hell; but, praise God, if we put our faith in Him, He has declared us "not guilty." He offers us eternal life and the power to overcome sin and do His will.

Verse 2: *"Because through Christ Jesus the law of the Spirit of life set me free from the law of sin and death."* The spirit of life is the Holy Spirit. 1 Corinthians 15:45 tells us, "The first man Adam became a living being; the last Adam, a life-giving Spirit." The last Adam is Christ. Christ rose from the dead and is, therefore, a life-giving Spirit. **Christ is a life-giving Spirit.** This is what Paul is saying in Romans 8:1. Many people were trying to be saved by keeping the Old Testament Law and they became tied up in all the rules, regulations, and the Jewish traditions. Who does this sound like? It sounds like most churches today. If we are focused on rules and regulations, we are not set free. When we trust Christ to save us, He removes the burden of trying to measure up and the guilt for never being able to.

Do you want to live a life of freedom? Turn to 2 Corinthians 3:17-18: "Where the Spirit of the Lord is, there is freedom." Not only does Christ give us life, He also gives us freedom. As we accept and understand God's truths, we are transformed into the likeness of Christ. Christ is a direct reflection of God. **Our transformation comes from our willingness to accept responsibility for our relationship with the Lord and our desire to know Him.** One key to the Christian life is to die to our self every day so that He can live in and through us. Another key is to live a spirit-led life. **This means to simply follow the Spirit of the Lord in every aspect of our life.** The more closely we follow Christ, the more we will be like Him.

Verse 3: *"For what the law was powerless to do in that it was weakened by the sinful nature, God did by sending his own Son in the likeness of sinful man to be a sin offering. And so he condemned sin in sinful man."* Jesus gave Himself as a "sin offering" – a sacrifice for our sins. In the Old Testament, animal sacrifices were continually offered at the temple. These sacrifices showed how serious the Israelites were about sin. Blood had to be shed for sins to be pardoned (Leviticus 17:11). But animal blood could not really atone for the sins of man. Hebrews 10:4 says, "It is impossible for the blood of bulls and goats to take away sins." These sacrifices were only a temporary way to deal with sin until Jesus came to take care of it permanently. Christ paid the penalty for all sins with His ultimate sacrifice on the cross.

Verse 5: *"Those who live according to the sinful nature have their minds set on what that nature desires; but those who live in accordance with the Spirit have their minds set on what the Spirit desires."* There are two types of people in the world: Those who are controlled by their sinful nature/themselves and those who are controlled by God. Those who try to control their own life will always be frustrated and eventually die a spiritual death; but those controlled by God's Spirit will live a life of joy and peace. Being controlled by the spirit doesn't mean everything will go your way, it doesn't mean you won't face problems and challenges in life. However it does mean that you will receive the divine peace and the divine power to work through whatever life throws your way. How do we allow the Spirit of Christ to control us?

1) <u>Let Go.</u> Give everything we have to the Lord. We are managers of what He has blessed us with.

2) <u>Come Clean.</u> Come clean before God – get honest, get real. We can't fool God.

3) <u>Die to Self.</u> Live one day at a time and die to self every day. Before we can truly live we must fully die to our old self.

4) <u>Pray.</u> Pray every morning before we start the day. Pray at every meal. Pray every night as we end the day. Pray for those in need. Prayer is simply talking to God – thanking Him, praising Him, giving our concerns over to Him, and asking Him to guide us.

5) <u>Read God's Word.</u> Meditate on it and apply it in daily living. Joshua Chapter 1 tells us how to be successful.

6) <u>Serve God for His Glory.</u> Get involved in church service. We are all agents of God on a mission to accomplish His work.

Verses 7-8: *"The sinful mind is hostile to God. It does not submit to God's law, nor can it do so. Those controlled by the sinful nature cannot please God."* Sin does not submit to the authority of God. James 4:4 says, "You adulterous people, don't you know that friendship with the world is hatred toward God? **Anyone who chooses to be a friend of the world becomes an enemy of God."** Pride is what leads us to be friends with the world. It makes us self-centered and makes us believe we are deserving of what the world offers. It creates greed. So, how can we kill pride? The Bible teaches us that we can overcome pride with humility through the power of Christ. We must recognize that everything about the wild, seductive life is phony. It's a cheap and short-term thrill ending in destruction. What God has to offer is much more. It's a life of eternal joy, which leads to deep, everlasting peace, and a love that transcends all things. Are you willing to totally embrace the Spirit of God and put Him in the driver's seat of your life?

CHAPTER 29
HOW TO RECOGNIZE A CHRISTIAN
Romans 8:9-15

"You, however, are controlled not by the sinful nature but by the Spirit, if the Spirit of God lives in you. And if anyone does not have the Spirit of Christ, he does not belong to Christ."- Romans 8:9

If it looks like a duck, walks like a duck, and quacks like a duck, then it must be a duck, right? However, many times things appear one way, but in reality they are totally different. Someone said, "Never believe what you hear and only half of what you see." This brings about a good theological question. How do you determine who is a real Christian? Am I a Christian because I say I am?

In the last chapter, we talked about the fact that the person who does not have Christ is controlled by his human nature, whereas God's Spirit directs the life of the believer. If you do not have the Spirit of Christ, you are not saved. In this chapter, Paul continues this line of thinking and gives us some fundamental principles to apply when examining our own lives.

One key principle for us to understand is that a believer is anyone who has the Spirit of God living in them. How do you know if the Spirit of God is living in you?

1) **You will believe that the Son of God is Jesus Christ and eternal life comes from Him.** 1 John 5:5 says, "Who is it that overcomes the world? Only he who believes that Jesus is the Son of God."

2) **Your life will express the characteristics of the Spirit of God.** Galatians 5:22 says, "But the fruit of the Spirit is love, joy, peace, patience, kindness, goodness, faithfulness."

3) **You know who the power source is.** Romans 8:26-27 says, "In the same way, the Spirit helps us in our weakness. We do not know what we ought to pray for, but the Spirit himself intercedes for us with groans that words cannot express. And he who searches our hearts knows the mind of the Spirit, because the Spirit intercedes for the saints in accordance with God's will."

4) **You will be empowered to serve the Lord and do His will.** Acts 1:8 says, "But you will receive power when the Holy Spirit comes on you; and you will be my witnesses in Jerusalem, and in all Judea and Samaria, and to the ends of the earth."

5) **You will become part of God's plan to build the church.** Ephesians 4:12-13 says, "To prepare God's people for works of service, so that the body of Christ may be built up until we all reach unity in the faith and in the knowledge of the Son of God and become mature, attaining to the whole measure of the fullness of Christ."

Verse 9: *"You, however, are controlled not by the sinful nature but by the Spirit, if the Spirit of God lives in you. And if anyone does not have the Spirit of Christ, he does not belong to Christ."* If God's Spirit lives in you, you are a Christian. Paul points his readers to the important fact that Satan has limited power, which impacts and influences the decisions we make each day. He defines the influence as "sinful nature." It is important for us to understand how our sinful nature affects our thoughts, desires, and ultimately, our actions. The emphasis in the verse is placed on the Spirit of Christ. This proves the point that we do not belong to ourselves. As Christians, we belong solely to Christ.

Verse 10: *"But if Christ is in you, your body is dead because of sin, yet your spirit is alive because of righteousness."* If Christ lives in you, then your old self has died, "yet because of the righteousness of Christ, your spirit becomes alive." Think of it this way: The body is the part of you where sin was born and it's the only part of you where sin can live. However, when we accept Christ in faith, we are transformed into a new person. The new person has a new power source, which is Christ. With Christ in us, our body has died. When the body dies, sin has nowhere to live. **This requires us to die to self each day so that sin cannot manifest itself in our bodies.**

Verse 11: *"And if the Spirit of him who raised Jesus from the dead is living in you, he who raised Christ from the dead will also give life to your mortal bodies through his Spirit, who lives in you."* Paul says here that the same Spirit that raised Jesus from the dead is the same Spirit that lives in us as Christians. The Holy Spirit is God's promise and guarantee of eternal life. 1 Thessalonians 4:14 says, "We believe that Jesus died and rose again and so we believe that God will bring with Jesus those who have fallen asleep in him." **Sin overpowers us as humans**. The sin disease corrupts every person. It degrades every individual. Sin steals our peace and joy and replaces them with trouble and pain. No person can escape the power of sin by their own effort. Sin causes us to be controlled by Satan. John 12:31 says, "Now is the time for judgment on this world; now the prince of this world will be driven out."

So, what is our only way out of this human problem? Every person must face a critical decision about himself. Who controls you: Satan or Christ? Every genuine Christian has God's own Spirit living in him. God's life-giving Spirit leads him to not be concerned with hatred, lying, cheating, stealing, boasting, resentment, and bitterness because those are ailments of a lost man. A saved man is interested in the things of God. A saved man is a humble man. **He does not need to boast or be praised because his security is in Christ.**

Verse 13: *"For if you live according to the sinful nature, you will die; but if by the Spirit you put to death the misdeeds of the body, you will live."* **If I do not allow Christ to kill sin, sin will kill me.** Sin is the problem and Christ is the answer. Our heart's desire should be to obey God and follow His will. Just because we act morally and live right does not mean we should feel good about our self. Doing good for the sake of making ourselves feel good rather than for giving God the credit is no good at all. Everything we do should be for the sake of Christ. **If it's important for us to get the credit for something we do, it is a reflection of pride and love of self, rather than humble and unconditional love.** Pride is controlling us when we believe we can control the secret sins of our life. Satan will attack us when we believe we are the most spiritually prepared. Anyone who thinks they have got it all together are most likely fooling themselves. Sometimes the easiest person to fool is our self. We can be doing all the right things with the wrong attitude and the wrong spirit and miss the whole purpose of Christian living, which is to simply live with the love of God's glory.

Verse 14: *"Because those who are led by the Spirit of God are sons of God."* Paul refers to those being led by the Spirit as "Sons of God." In Roman culture, an adopted person lost all his rights with his old family and gained new rights with the new family who had adopted him. So he became a full heir to his new father's estate. When we come to Christ, we gain the privilege that goes with being a child of God. **We receive the same inheritance as Christ.** We become sons of God.

Verse 15: *"For you did not receive a spirit that makes you a slave again to fear, but you received the Spirit of sonship. And by him we cry, 'Abba, Father.'"* As God's children, we should not fear, but be joyful because we will share in the treasures of heaven.

Here are five ways to kill sin in your life through the power of Christ:

1) **Confess your sins to God in prayer.** The first step is for us to come clean with God. Until we are real, He cannot be real in our lives.

2) **Set your heart on God.** When you set your heart on the Lord, you live for Him and you build a strong defense against Satan.

3) **Meditate on God's Word.** Make time daily to study and read God's Word. Read for quality, not quantity. Apply the Scriptures to your life in a practical way.

4) **Get on your knees in prayer.** If you're on your knees, you will not have far to fall. A person on their knees before God is an act of submission to the Lordship of Christ. Most of the time, I'm sure God is pleased when we go to our knees in love for Him, without begging for Him to resolve some huge issue in our life.

5) **Be obedient to God.** God wants us to walk with Him. He does not want you to try and negotiate a deal with Him such as, "Lord, if you will just give me a blessing, I will give you 25% of the blessing." The question is, "How much are you giving now?" Obedience is far more important than any sacrifice you try to make.

So the question is this: What is keeping you from allowing God to become real in your life?

CHAPTER 30
WE ARE OBLIGATED TO
LIVE BY THE SPIRIT
Romans 8:10-13

"Therefore, brothers, we have an obligation—but it is not to the sinful nature, to live according to it. For if you live according to the sinful nature, you will die; but if by the Spirit you put to death the misdeeds of the body, you will live."- Romans 8:12-13

Have you ever considered what the Christian life would be without the presence of the Holy Spirit? When I travel to Brazil to work with Brazilians, we build chapels, community centers, medical clinics, vocational schools and the key ingredient in all of the projects is concrete. It's a material of strength and durability. To make concrete requires sand, rock, water, and cement. All of the ingredients are critical to the process of making concrete; however, **the key ingredient is cement.** Without cement, all the other materials have no structural strength. In our spiritual lives, the Holy Spirit is the key ingredient for us to live a life in Christ.

Other questions might be, "Is the Holy Spirit present in your life? Do you really understand the role of the Holy Spirit? What does He do? What is His purpose?" In the last chapter, we discussed that there are two kinds of people in the world: Those controlled by their sinful nature and those controlled by the Holy Spirit. If the Holy Spirit is not in control of your life, you are going in the wrong direction. Instead, you are like many people who think just because they say "yes" to Christ they do not have to live for Christ. This is a fundamental flaw in our country's culture today. Paul says that living for Christ is the evidence that we have the Holy Spirit.

The truth is that Satan wants us to believe that we can live any way we want as long as we do not harm anyone. Paul says that's not true. In verse 12, Paul says that "we have an obligation, but it is not to the sinful nature." As Christians, our obligation is "to live by the Spirit and put to death the mistakes of the body" (v. 13). A holy life comes from the Spirit. Without the Spirit, we are not truly alive. If we are truly honest with ourselves, living for ourselves brings us only a temporary pleasure; but, deep inside, we lack the true peace that can only come from a relationship with Christ.

Wouldn't it be awful to come before God on Judgment Day and hear Him say, "My son, you were saved as a child, but you wasted all those years doing what you wanted to do, never asking what I wanted you to do"? As Christians we belong to God in Christ. God wants us to live in the power of His Holy Spirit. His Spirit is our teacher, our mentor, our advocate, our connection to God, our guidance, and our direction.

Back in verse 11, the Holy Spirit also guarantees eternal life for those who trust in Him. The Holy Spirit is in us by faith and, by faith, we are certain to live with Christ forever. In Galatians 5:24, Paul says, "Those who belong to Christ Jesus have crucified the sinful nature with its passions and desires." What Paul is saying is that if we have truly, in faith, received the free gift of salvation in Christ, then the power of God's Spirit, along with our free will, declares, "It's time to kill my past." There comes a time in everyone's life when we must draw a line in the sand. We are either totally for God in Christ or we are not. If we are, God will give us the power and the courage to kill and bury our past. Maybe some of us are allowing our past to control us. But, the cool thing about God is that He loves us so much, He's just waiting for us to come back to Him and say, "Lord, forgive me. Lord, restore me. I want to know You more. Lord, I want to bury all of my past and start afresh, and have a new life with You."

This is what most of us have to do at some point in our lives. It happened with me when I was 28 years old. I was a Christian, but I really was not living my life for Christ. I was not allowing Christ to guide and direct me. It took an overseas mission trip for me to see what a wonderful God I serve. God used a mission trip 5,000 miles away from home to show me His love for me. God radically transformed my way of life. From that point, God began to change me and help me understand His will for my life and, even today, He continues to shape and mold me into the person He wants me to be. Will you consider allowing Christ to become, not only your Savior, but also the Lord of your life? We will never be perfect. Each of us will struggle in different areas, but as we allow Christ to rule and reign in our life, we will find an inner peace and inner strength that can only exist when He is present.

CHAPTER 31
BELIEVERS SHARE IN GOD'S GLORY
Romans 8:17

"Now if we are children, then we are heirs—heirs of God and co-heirs with Christ, if indeed we share in his sufferings in order that we may also share in his glory."- Romans 8:17

In the mid-90's, I had the chance to spend time with a man named David. David was a man who truly walked by faith each day. He had a great job as an airline pilot for one of the major airlines. The Lord called him to start his own ministry. He quit his job and started a ministry preaching to people on the streets by painting the gospel with florescent paint and black lights. My missionary friend, Wade Akins, was taught the same technique and he and I traveled to many cities in the country of Brazil showing the Jesus film and holding paint talks. One night after a crusade, David and I were talking and I asked him what was important for me, as a Christian, to know. He said, "Never touch God's glory. God's glory belongs to Him and He gives it to us because of our love for Him. If we touch it, if we exploit it, we ruin the purpose of His glory."

This chapter deals with the fact that God's Holy Spirit guarantees us glory because of our salvation in Christ. As believers, we are no longer held hostage to sin. While sin still approaches us and affects each of us every day, we are able to overcome it when we trust the Lord and discipline our lives to follow His will. **God has given me the best of what He's got because of His love for me.** God's Son was the most significant thing he could have ever sacrificed. He not only gave us His Son, but He gave us the Holy Spirit, forgiveness, and eternal life. He wants us to ask Him for whatever we need. Many of us may be in difficult situations today. God's Word tells us that He will provide us with what we need. When I think of this I am reminded of the title of the old spiritual gospel hymn, "Just Hold On, Help is On the Way".

Verse 17: *"Now if we are children, then we are heirs – heirs of God and co-heirs with Christ, if indeed we share in his sufferings in order that we may also share in his glory."* In other words, Paul makes a clear distinction that *since* we are God's children, *then* we are also His heirs. For us to really understand what he is saying, we must evaluate his audience: the Romans. Roman law and Jewish law were two totally different types of systems. For example, in the Jewish tradition, the eldest son received a double portion of the family's inheritance, but in the Roman culture every person in the family, even those who were adopted received an equal share of the inheritance.

How do we know we are God's children? Let's jump back just a moment to verse 16: *"The Spirit himself testifies with our spirit that we are God's children."* When we become Christians, we gain the same rights as if we were children in the Roman culture of God. One of the most powerful privileges that we are given is the Holy Spirit. Paul gives us insight into how God's Spirit works in us in Galatians 4:5-6: "But when the time had fully come, God sent his Son, born of a woman, born under law, to redeem those under law, that we might receive the full rights of sons. Because you are sons, God sent the Spirit of his Son into our hearts, the Spirit who calls out, 'Abba, Father.'"

Now let's go back to verse 17b: *"If we indeed share in His sufferings in order that we may also share in His glory."* **There is a price to pay for being a Christian**. Paul talks about his sufferings. In the first century, they faced economic challenges, social persecution, and even death for being Christians. What suffering do we face today as Christians in America? As we know, we are under constant pressure to conform to the world's standards. When we make a stand to follow Christ we feel the most pressure from the world. But let's closely examine the last part of 17b: "That we may also share in His glory." The Holy Spirit guarantees our glory. Can God be glorified without our suffering? **There can be no glory without suffering**. Every issue that is causing us to suffer today, God wants to use for His glory through us as believers. Most of us look at suffering as awful. Paul viewed it as an opportunity to bring God glory. **If we view suffering as awful, it's a clear indication that we are focused on ourselves rather than on Christ.** God will use circumstances and situations to grow us into maturity. Justification is the beginning of salvation and glorification is the completion of salvation.

Before Adam's fall, he was sinless. He radiated the glory of God because he was created in the image of God. But when Adam fell, he lost his glory and became a sinful creature. Romans 3:23 tells us "For all have sinned and fall short of the glory of God." **When we stop and really think about it, most of us try to gain glory for ourselves, apart from God.** This is always a futile attempt to achieve self-esteem that inevitably ends in frustration and giving up. My point is that the ultimate purpose of salvation is to forgive and to cleanse people of their sin and to restore them to God's glory. The glory we receive through Christ's sacrifice is greater than the glory Adam received in his innocence.

Really, our deal in heaven is much better than the deal we get here on earth. Normally, if we receive an inheritance, we would receive a proportional amount, a pro rata share. John 17:17 says **that we will receive the same glory as Christ and become one with Him.** Because of our faith and salvation, we share a joint inheritance with Christ. Titus 3:7 says we are "justified by His grace [in order that] we might be made heirs according to the hope of eternal life." Here's the bottom-line: If you and I, as Christians, are not anticipating the second coming of Christ and living in accordance with His will, we are tied to the things of the world. Before we can truly serve the Lord we must be set free from the things of the world. Until we identify ourselves as citizens of heaven ("But our citizenship is in heaven. And we eagerly await a Savior from there, the Lord Jesus Christ." Philippians 3:20), the hope and expectation of sharing in God's glory should lead us to dedicate ourselves to living for Him. The challenge for all of us is to know that God's Spirit guarantees us glory and that what really counts is Christ living in us, not us working our way to heaven.

CHAPTER 32
THE LIFE TO COME
Romans 8:18-25

"I consider that our present sufferings are not worth comparing with the glory that will be revealed in us."- Romans 18:8

We were told in a previous chapter that all true Christians have received "the spirit of adoption." All Christians. Not members of a certain denomination. Not those who have been dunked or poured or sprinkled. Not those who have made overt declarations. But those who are true Christians at heart are adopted into the household of God. They become sons of God through Christ the Son. They receive a new spiritual and divine life from God through Christ, and that life reflects the glory of its source. We who are true Christians are daily becoming more like Jesus in our walk, in our talk, in our family life, in our church life, in the very fiber of our being. This chapter concerns what the Bible tells us about the physical body and its fate:

1) The body still remains a source of weakness.

2) The body is weak because it is the seat of sin.

3) The body is sluggish and unsuitable for high purposes.

4) The body still remains subject to the Law of sin and death.

5) The body is not eternal like the Father who breathed into it the breath of life.

6) The body remains in bondage and has not yet received the adoption.

The verses we are looking at today, in harmony with Paul's whole message, look forward to a change in the body. These verses show the future relations to the renewed spirit as the crown and climax of the work of redemption and declare that until that change is effected, Christians wait and groan in anticipation for their adoption. In the words of that old Negro spiritual: "I'm going to wait, until my change comes."

Let us note that a future bodily life is needed in order to give definiteness and solidity to the concept of immortality. The gospel has made the idea of a future state infinitely more believable and more powerful mainly because of its emphatic proclamation of an actual resurrection and a future bodily life. The gospel teaches and proclaims that there will be a resurrection day and that we will have a place in the kingdom of God. Proof of immortality in the gospel is drawn from the historical fact of the resurrection of Jesus Christ and of His ascension in bodily form into heaven. It is this concept that gives the gospel its power and transforms a vague and shadowy conception of immortality into a solid faith, for which we already have an historical guarantee.

The thought of the future life as a bodily life satisfies the longings of the heart. One of the reasons we shrink away from the thought of death comes from unwillingness to part with an old companion and friend – our body. All ideas of the future that do not indicate a bodily life open up a ghastly and uninviting vision of existence, which cannot but repel those who are accustomed to the fellowship of their bodies. The body that will be resurrected is an emancipated body. It is free. We have to interpret "the resurrection of the body" by the definite apostolic declaration. There are opposing differences in our finite body and the eternal body we will one day inhabit.

1) One is sown in corruption and the other is raised in incorruption.

2) One is sown in dishonor and the other is raised in glory.

146

3) One is sown in weakness and the other is raised in power.

4) One is sown a natural body and the other is raised a spiritual body.

We must also look at Paul's other representation of this idea in chapter 5 of 2 Corinthians. Here he uses two images to show the contrast between the corporeal, temporary body and the body of glory, which belongs to the future life.

1) The earthly house of this tabernacle – a clay hut, which lasts but for a time.

2) The house of God made not with hands, which is eternal in the heavens.

We know that our present body is imperfect; it deteriorates, it is faulty. The redeemed body will be a more perfect instrument for communication with the eternal God. That body, which is the fit instrument of the spirit, may become its means of knowing more deeply, thinking more wisely, understanding more swiftly, comprehending more widely, remembering more firmly, and judging more soundly. The redeemed body will have in it nothing to tempt and nothing to confuse, but will be a helper to the Spirit and a source of strength to the weak.

The redeemed body is a consequence of Christ's indwelling Spirit. The Christian, in his regenerated spirit, has been born again. The Christian longs for a time when the regenerated spirit will no longer dwell in the clay cottage of this tabernacle, but will inhabit a congruous dwelling in the eternal, heavenly house of God. If the Spirit of God that raised Jesus from the dead dwells in you, He shall also quicken your mortal bodies by that same Spirit. The resurrection is promised for all mankind, but for some it may be a resurrection towards endless living and no glory, nor any beauty or blessedness. The fact is you are going to be resurrected. How do you wish to live for eternity? The sole way leading to the resurrection of glory is the way of faith in Jesus Christ. If we yield ourselves to Him:

1) He will place His Spirit in our spirit.

2) He will guide and increasingly sanctify us through life.

3) He will deliver us by the indwelling of the Spirit of life from the Law of sin and death.

When it comes to thinking about death, let us all follow Paul's example. This man of God was cheerful about the prospect of death. To Paul, death was not an enemy but a friend because he knew it meant being at home with the Lord. Have you thought about death? All of us will one day die, but in Christ we are promised a new body and a new house.

CHAPTER 33
THE HOLY SPIRIT INTERCEDES
Romans 8:26-27

"In the same way, the Spirit helps us in our weakness. We do not know what we ought to pray for, but the Spirit himself intercedes for us with groans that words cannot express."- Romans 8:26

This chapter talks about how, we as believers receive an intercessory connection from the Holy Spirit. Have you ever been so weak you simply did not know what to do? Have you ever tried to pray and you just couldn't? As Christians, God has designed for us a relief valve that engages when we are about to give up hope. This relief comes in the form of the Holy Spirit. One of God's promises is that He will give us the resources to cope with our problems. Even when we don't know what to pray, the Holy Spirit will intercede for us and let God know what we need. If we pray for God's will to be done and trust God for the outcome, He promises to be there for us in the process. Oftentimes, there is a gap between our expectations and what God has in store for us.

We learned in verses 19-20, "The creation waits in eager expectation for the sons of God to be revealed." In verses 23-25, Paul tells us, "Believers groan." Now we find that the Holy Spirit groans. Verses 26 and 27 inform us, *"The Spirit Himself intercedes for us with groans that words cannot express."* Creation groans. The believer groans. The Holy Spirit groans.

In these verses, we find the Holy Spirit signing over the undesirable "fallenness" of man, the earth, and the universe. Verse 21 tells us, "The creation itself will be liberated from its bondage to decay and brought into the glorious freedom of the children of God." Verse 19 says, "The creation waits in eager expectation for the sons of God to be revealed." And we come then to verses 26 and 27: *"In the same way, the Spirit helps us in our weakness. We do not know what we ought to pray for, but the Spirit himself intercedes for us with groans that words cannot express. And he who searches our hearts knows the mind of the Spirit, because the Spirit intercedes for the saints in accordance with God's will."*

This section finishes up our look at the inexpressible groans for glory, the groaning of the Holy Spirit. This section is so profound it is difficult for us to fully understand the benefits. It is an amazing encouragement because what it says is that, as believers who are sensing the weight of our "fallenness," who are groaning in these human bodies, who are waiting for the ultimate redemption of our body, our souls have been redeemed.

We are waiting for the redeemed body, aren't we? We're waiting to get out of our flesh, our "fallenness," and enter into glory. Paul says that the Spirit of God is in us groaning for the same thing. We are secure in the purpose of the Son. We are secure in the progress and power of the Spirit, as He too longs that we would be glorified through Him. Just like we groan, the Spirit does also. When we become a Christian, it's so wonderful to know God's on our side. Our "fallenness" and our humanness are as much a concern of the Spirit of God as they are our concern.

Can I keep myself saved? No. Who's going to keep me saved then? The Spirit of God. That's His unique work. He intercedes on our behalf, along with the Lord Jesus Christ. The Spirit tends to our infirmities. That's a comprehensive word. It simply means "our weaknesses," our "fallenness." Not just our weak prayers, but also our whole weak existence, our whole human problem of being in this flesh, this mortal body, this sinful state. How can we keep ourselves saved? We can't, because we don't even know what to pray for. That's such an important truth. And I don't know that Christians really understand this fundamental spiritual truth.

You see this is the problem. When we have taught in years past about eternal security, we sort of say, "Well, if you're saved, you're saved forever." And we have agreed that that is, in fact, true. But we have missed somehow the marvelous corresponding truth that we are guaranteed that eternal security because of the continual intercessory work of the Son and the Spirit. And so we should be offering praise to the Son who intercedes on our behalf and prays for us when Satan would have us. And we should also be grateful that the Spirit of God helps us in our weakness. We couldn't remain saved ourselves unless the Divine Intercessor stood for us before the throne of God. This is a great truth. Hebrews 7:25, do you remember that verse? "Therefore he is able to save completely those who come to God through him, because he always lives to intercede for them." What does it mean to be saved completely? It means to be saved to the epitome, to the limits. It means that from the moment of salvation to the moment of Glory, we are saved completely. How is this possible? "He always lives to intercede for them."

What keeps us saved is the ever-living, interceding Christ, for such a High Priest was fitting for us. We not only have Christ in heaven interceding for us, but we have the Holy Spirit in us interceding for us. We have a faithful High Priest, who is Christ, in heaven and we have a faithful High Priest, who is Christ, in our hearts, for the Spirit Himself makes intercession. The same word is used of Christ in Hebrews, **"For us."** We could never attain to glory. We could never pray our way through, because we don't even know how to pray to protect our self in spiritual conflict. And so we have help from the Savior in heaven and the Spirit on earth. It's obvious we don't know what to pray for, isn't it? In 2 Corinthians 12, Paul prayed three times for the Lord to remove the thorn in his flesh. Three times the Lord did what? Nothing. He didn't remove it. And Paul finally decided that whatever state he was in, he would be content. And he learned what all of us should know. We really don't know what to pray for. We don't know how to pray for things we ought to pray for. As humans, we are so weak.

The Holy Spirit makes intercession. What does that mean? Basically it means to rescue someone who is in trouble and who has no resources to escape. This is why Satan continues to work so furiously on believers and to attack so furiously those who name the name of Christ. Satan knows that we are being kept by the power of Christ and the power of the Spirit, so he wars against the

Spirit and the living Christ, every way he can, so that he may at some point, debilitate their work. Therefore, we know that Christ is not, having died on the cross and risen to heaven, just kicking back and watching everything sort of fall into line. No, he is working to uphold all things, including redemptive things, and the Spirit of God is not finished. He didn't all of a sudden stop doing things when the age of miracles ended at the Apostolic era. No, he makes intercession. He pleads to the power of God. He comes to us with power to rescue us when we have no resource for rescue. And would you notice there's an emphasis in verse 26, **"The Spirit Himself."** It's His work.

The Holy Spirit sees and understands our weakness, that not only do we sin, but we don't even know how to pray to defend ourselves. And the blessed Holy Spirit in us yearns for our glory. He yearns for our being in the image of Christ. This is the heart of God the Father. This is the heart of God the Son. This is the heart of God the Spirit. The Spirit of God is working in us to bring about the perfect will of God in a sustained effort. The Spirit of God works to produce the end result.

Now let's go to verse 27. In the previous passage, we have the Spirit interceding for us. Verse 27 says, *"And He who searches our hearts knows the mind of the Spirit."* Who is it that searches our hearts? The Lord reveals His thought process in 1 Samuel 16:17: "Man looks at the outward appearance, but the Lord looks at the heart." Psalm 139:1-2 says, "Oh Lord, you have searched me and you know me. You know when I sit and when I rise; you perceive my thoughts from afar." Acts 1:24 tells us, "Lord, you know everyone's heart." And Romans 8:27a says, "And He who searches our hearts knows the mind of the Spirit." That's God. That's just a name for God, the heart searcher. He knows the mind of the Spirit. The Spirit intercedes for us and God in His holiness hears it. And then this, "Because the Spirit intercedes for the Saints in accordance with God's will" (v. 27b). You do not know the will of God. He does. You may not know how to pray. He does. Do you know what it means to "pray in the Spirit"? It means to pray according to the will of God. God always knows what the Spirit is praying "because He's always praying in accordance with His will."

So the Spirit intercedes according to God's will, the Son intercedes according to God's will, and God hears and understands all their intercession and responds. It is by their interceding ministries that we are kept. So, when some guy comes along and says, "Well, I believe you can lose your salvation," he strikes a blast against the work of the Savior and the work of the Spirit. That is not just some small disagreement in the church. That is to question the power of the Son of God and the Spirit of God.

God hears the Spirit. The Spirit always prays according to the will of God. This is cool stuff. Will you begin to use the tools you have in your spiritual tool box? Reach in and grasp the greatest resource available to us – the Holy Spirit.

CHAPTER 34
WHERE DOES GOD WORK?
Romans 8:28-30

"And we know that in all things God works for the good of those who love him, who have been called according to his purpose." -
Romans 8:28

This chapter contains arguably the greatest promise we can find in the Bible. It's a promise that allows us as simple laymen to find rest. It's a promise that God gives to all His children. Verse 28: *"And we know that in all things God works for the good of those who love him, who have been called according to His purpose."* I want to break this verse down into specific components so we can closely examine what Paul is communicating to the Church of Rome.

1) **"And we know."** Paul is stating with absolute clarity that God's Word is truth. To say that you "know" something means that you know it to be fact. Paul is saying that eternal security is clearly revealed to us by God so that we, as believers, are able to know with certainty that we can take God at His Word. Here's the question: Do you really know? Do you know for sure your salvation is secure? Paul had a divine understanding of how God's redemptive plan works. He knew that, because of God's faithfulness, his salvation was secure.

2) **"That in all things God works for the good of those who love him."** Let me ask you a question: If CitiGroup Bank guarantees a $10 billion dollar loan, what does that mean in the financial world? Is it really guaranteed to be paid? No – we have all seen the current debacle involving some of the largest companies in the world. Is anything really totally 100%

guaranteed in the financial world? No! But, what if I told you that God was going to guarantee the loan? What would you think? Yes, if God is the guarantor, you are guaranteed your money. Why? Because He has never failed to meet a promise. **God does the work.** We come to Him in faith, realizing our brokenness. We cannot fix ourselves. Only God can fix us. What did He work out? **"All"** things. What does "all things" mean? "All things" is all-inclusive; it means no qualifications, no limits, no restrictions, and no conditions. Let me say that this promise is conditional, however. The promise is based on us loving God. The Bible teaches that we can know a person loves God by their obedience to Him. A person cannot say only with their mouth they love God. Love is an action, not just a word. Therefore, our love is proven through our life, not by what we say.

3) **"Neither height nor depth, nor anything else in all creation, will be able to separate us from the love of God that is in Christ Jesus our Lord."** (Romans 8:39) Notice God is not saying that He prevents His children from experiencing things that can harm them. He is saying that He has the power to take terrible, awful, painful experiences and use them to His glory and to our eventual benefit. Let's look at 2 Corinthians 7-10. When we suffer, God will use it for our benefit. So if **"in all things God works for the good of those who love him,"** the working is of God's doing, not ours. You see, God's power and God's will are superior to anything we can imagine. Do you believe in God's power? Do you believe God works in all things for good? What does that really mean? It means that the Lord can take whatever course you're on and turn it into a path of loving kindness and truth so that He will be glorified. God's goodness and faithfulness work to the good of His people. God's Word is for our good. James 1:2-3 says, "Consider it pure joy, my brothers, whenever you face trials of many kinds." 1 Peter 1:7 says, "These have come so that your faith – of greater

worth than gold, which perishes even though refined by fire – may be proved genuine." 2 Corinthians 12:9-10 says, "That is why, for Christ's sake, I delight in weaknesses, in insults, in hardships, in persecutions, in difficulties. For when I am weak, then I am strong." Strength comes from being broken; strength comes from surviving the difficulties of life. **The more problems we have, the more we must learn to depend on God; when we depend on God, that's when we find true strength.**

You see, hardships and suffering can teach us more about our true self than anything else in the world. Life trials cause us to learn valuable lessons that could never be learned any other way. Suffering causes us to develop true humility and build true character. There's a difference between false humility and true humility. The truly humble person is someone who is transparent and who has a compassion for others, regardless of who they are.

One year during Christmas, I made an interesting observation when our Bible study group was ringing the bell for the Salvation Army in front of the Hobby Lobby store in Jackson, TN. I noticed that more poor people gave money to charity than wealthy people. I asked myself this question: Why would a poor person give up the money he has to help someone that he's never met? Why do they give when they have so little? Why did those people who have money ignore us most of the time? The answer is that the poor person can identify with the pain of other people and the rich person cannot, unless the rich person was once poor. The more a person has the more independent he becomes. It's difficult to be wealthy and grasp the depth of true dependence on the Lord. I prayed just the other night for the first time, "God, thank you for my pain because I can see that you have changed me. When I become weak is when I become more dependent on You."

Pain causes us to examine ourselves closely and, for men, pride is a big factor. Men, God tells us that all of these things work together for the good of those who love Him. Even the person you think is the sorriest on the planet, God can use for His good.

Matthew 12:30 says, "He who is not with me is against me." A genuine love for God is a personal connection with Him and a desire to know Him. A genuine love for God is displayed in a person's daily actions of trusting in His power, being sensitive and obedient to His will, wanting to please Him, having a love for His people, and hating evil. I challenge you today to commit your life to following Him and trusting in Him. Will you take a chance and trust Him even if it feels uncomfortable?

CHAPTER 35
PREDESTINATION
Romans 8:29-30

"For those God foreknew he also predestined to be conformed to the likeness of his Son, that he might be the firstborn among many brothers. And those he predestined, he also called; those he called, he also justified; those he justified, he also glorified."
- Romans 8:29

This chapter deals with the subject of predestination. This is a matter that theologians have debated for centuries. Some believe that God specifically chose certain people to receive His gift of salvation. They point to Ephesians 1:11 that says, "In him we were also chosen, having been predestined according to the plan of him who works out everything in conformity with the purpose of his will." Others believe that God foreknew those who would respond to Him, and upon those He set His mark (predestined). The word "predestined" means "marked beforehand". This is another way of saying that God's redemptive mark is God's doing, not ours. Because of His unlimited and infinite love, God has adopted us as His children. We don't deserve adoption, but due to His love for us, He has graced us with a means to be included into His family. God's grace is His voluntary, loving favor given to those who He saves by acceptance in faith. Salvation is not earned, nor is it deserved. No intellectual or moral effort can gain the grace of God because it comes solely from God's mercy and love. Without the grace of God, no person can be saved. To receive it we must acknowledge and realize that we cannot save ourselves, that only God can save us and that the only way to receive His love and forgiveness is through faith in Christ. This is what I know to be true:

    1) God's purpose for people was not an after-thought; it was designed by Christ before the foundation of the world.

2) God sent His only Son, Jesus Christ, for the sake of all mankind, not just a select few.

3) God knows all things, He is sovereign. With God there is no scale of time. Thousands of years are like seconds to Him, therefore, His being is multi-dimensional to the extent we will never understand His full omnipresence. His power is unlimited; therefore, He has the ability to know and to do all things within the confines of His Word. However, because He knows all things does not mean He holds back His unconditional love or limits His atonement of the sins of all men. Man's sins are atoned for those who accept Him in faith. Christ came to set "all" men free from the bondage of sin. We cannot place ourselves in the same position of God. In my view, to say that God predestined those who will go to heaven and those who will go to hell does not represent a true biblical perspective. If one takes this position, we are merely God's puppets, totally controlled by Him. On the other hand, the person who takes the position that man can work his way to salvation, also does not have a true biblical perspective. The choice of man does not mean his will to choose is superior to God's sovereignty. Both positions are extreme and grounded by man's philosophical speculation and create confusion for most believers.

4) God uses His Holy Spirit to draw all men to Himself. The Holy Spirit plays an important role in the process. Some believe man's will is just as important as God's sovereignty; I do not share this view. Others believe God's sovereignty means man does not have a choice; I do not share this view either. Our part is to accept the free gift of salvation in faith or reject it. God never forces His love on us. He allows us to make the ultimate decision. We choose to simply believe and have faith in Him or not. If He forced us to believe in Him, His love would become conditional.

160

5) Man's will is always secondary to the sovereignty of God, simply because of the hierarchy of God. While God's Spirit urges one to a point of salvation, it is man's ultimate decision to accept or reject Christ. Many of these issues will remain a mystery until we are together with the Lord. For a person to say he has all the answers is spiritually unhealthy. I know because I've been that person. What I do know is this: God's love is eternal. His wisdom and power are supreme. Upon our accepting Him as Lord, He will always guide and protect us until the day we stand in His presence. God's love is for "all." God's Son came to set "all" men free and since we are unable to process and comprehend His power, we must put our total trust in Him and assume His promises are totally true.

Verse 29: *"For those God foreknew he also predestined to be conformed to the likeness of his Son, that he might be the firstborn among many brothers."* The conforming part is called "sanctification," which means "becoming like Christ" or "to be declared holy." When we accept the truth of forgiveness through Christ as the sacrificial death, we are accepting God's Word as truth, therefore, the truth sanctifies us and we are cleansed from our sin (John 17:17).

Verse 30: *"And those he predestined, he also called; those he called, he also justified; those he justified, he also glorified."* Paul outlines a series of steps to gain insight into the process of a believer. The following are the basic concepts Paul refers to in Romans to explain salvation in Christ:

1) **Election:** (Romans 9:10-13) God's choice for a specific task or destiny. For example, God chose Israel. God elects that all men be drawn unto Him, but He recognizes that all men will not accept His gift of salvation.

161

2) **Predestination:** (Romans 8:29) Does God know who will be saved? Yes, but His knowing does not interfere with our choosing to accept Him in faith.

3) **Justification:** (Romans 4:25) God's act of declaring us "not guilty" for our sins.

4) **Atonement:** (Romans 3:25) The removal of God's punishment for sin through the perfect sacrifice of His Son, Jesus Christ.

5) **Redemption:** (Romans 8:23) Redemption is the price paid for freedom. Jesus redeemed those who accept Him in faith by His death on the cross.

6) **Sanctification:** (Romans 5:2) Becoming more like Christ through the work of the Holy Spirit. To empty and fill the void in our lives with Christ is the process of sanctification.

7) **Glorification:** (Romans 8:18) This is the ultimate state of the believer after death, when we become like Christ (1 John 3:2).

CHAPTER 36
SUBSTITUTIONARY ATONEMENT
Romans 8:31-38

*"He who did not spare his own Son, but gave him up for us all—
how will he not also, along with him, graciously give us all
things?"*- Romans 8:32

Paul closes chapter 8 of Romans with what many Bible
scholars call the **"Hymn of Security."** Paul addresses serious
questions to relevant issues of that day. One of the main questions
was **"Can a person lose their salvation?"**

Verse 31: *"What then shall we say in response to this?"*
Here, Paul is addressing the doctrine of substitutionary atonement.
However, the main focus of his point is related to the security of
Christ's atonement. Let's stop here just a moment and break down
the doctrine of substitutionary atonement. What does
substitutionary mean? It means something put in the place of
something else. God put His only Son into our place for the
atonement of our sins. What does atonement mean? Because man
cannot become righteous on his own, God graciously provided His
redemption through the atoning sacrifice of His Son, Jesus Christ.
"To atone" means "to reconcile, to make amends for an offense."
For every offense there is a certain penalty. Our offense is our sin.
Christ atones for our sin or reconciles the offense of our sin with
His death on the cross. He exchanged His life for ours. He took our
place; therefore, He was the substitutionary atonement.

When a person embraces Christ in repentant faith, Christ,
who is the sinless, perfect Son of God, satisfies for us our sins and
makes us eternally at peace. This is a critical point for us to
understand and grasp, because we must know that Christ did our
work for us on the cross. In others words, the atoning work of
Christ is the basis for our assurance - the assurance of our
salvation. When we are eternally secure, then we are free to focus

163

on Christ and His goodness and move our focus away from our own goodness. We are able to serve the Lord with the confidence that nothing can separate us from the love of God. When we know our salvation is secure, we begin to know a peace that deepens our faith in Christ. God gave us His only Son as a testimony of His love for us. Jesus not only paid the price for your sins, but also for the sins of the entire world. 1 John 2:1-2 says, "My dear children, I write this to you so that you will not sin. But if anybody does sin, we have one who speaks to the Father in our defense – Jesus Christ, the Righteous One. He is the atoning sacrifice for our sins, and not only for ours but also for the sins of the whole world."

Verse 31b: *"If God is for us, who can be against us?"* The Greek translation literally says, **"Because God is with us."** If anyone could rob us of our salvation, they would be greater than God. God is the giver of salvation and He is the sustainer of salvation. Paul is asking if there is anyone stronger than God? David had an unreserved confidence in the Lord. In Psalm 27:1 he says, "The Lord is my light and my salvation -whom shall I fear?" Jesus was the sacrifice for you and me on the cross. There are two unchangeable features of God's constant purpose – His promise and His oath to honor that promise. God is not looking for a perfect faith, but He does want us to have an authentic faith, an undeniable dependence on Christ.

CHAPTER 37
THE HOLY SPIRIT AS YOUR GUIDE
Romans 9:1-15

"I speak the truth in Christ—I am not lying, my conscience confirms it in the Holy Spirit."- Romans 9:1

In chapters 9-11 of Romans we will discover some of the most fascinating passages in the New Testament. This section is filled with practical doctrine and marked by a focus on Israel. Paul had a passion for the lost and a great concern for the nation of Israel. In Romans 9:1-3, Paul shares his deep love for the Jews, both as a nation and as individuals.

Verse 1: *"I speak the truth in Christ–I am not lying."* He begins by assuring the Jews of his personal honesty. In other words, he wants them to know that what he is about to say is absolutely true. Paul presents three witnesses that back up the credibility of what he is saying:

1) **Christ:** He calls on his Lord and Savior, Jesus Christ, as an undisputable witness.

2) **His Conscience:** Paul tells us his "conscience confirms" that what he is about to say is true. Our conscience can be a reliable guide if we have our mind filled with the Word of God and have a biblical worldview. Martin Luther, the reformer, said, "My conscience is captive to the Word of God." However, our conscience can also guide us in the wrong direction. It can be trained to do wrong or it can be trained to do good. Titus 1:15 says, "To the pure, all things are pure, but to those who are corrupted and do not believe, nothing is pure. In fact, both their minds and consciences are corrupted."

3) **The Holy Spirit:** The Holy Spirit dwells in every
   believer and guides a Christian's heart.

Verse 2: *"I have great sorrow and unceasing anguish in my
heart."* Here Paul makes very clear his love and passion for the
Jewish people.

Verse 3-4a: *"For I could wish that I myself were cursed
and cut off from Christ for the sake of my brothers, those of my
own race, the people of Israel."* Again, we can see Paul's passion
for the Jews. It was his great love for the lost that made him such a
powerful instrument in the hands of God. The word "cursed" here
means "going to hell." He was willing to go to hell if it would
mean that the Jews would be saved. We can see the same passion
in Moses in Exodus 32:32: "But now, please forgive their sin – but
if not, then blot me out of the book you have written." This reveals
unbelievable leadership combined with love and courage for those
who are lost.

Do you have a passion to reach the lost like the Apostle
Paul? When was the last time you shared the gospel with a non-
Christian with the purpose of leading him or her to Christ? If you
have lacked this passion, why not pray and ask God to give it to
you now? Ask Him to help you bring lost men and women to
Christ and to use your life for His glory.

CHAPTER 38
GOD'S CHOSEN PEOPLE
Romans 9:16-29

*"As he says in Hosea: 'I will call them "my people" who are not
my people; and I will call her "my loved one" who is not my loved
one,' and, 'It will happen that in the very place where it was said
to them, "You are not my people," they will be called "sons of the
living God."* - Romans 9:25-26

This chapter focuses on the blessings of the Israelites –
God's chosen people. The Bible tells us that they were blessed to
be Israelites, or "people of Israel." This means that they were
descendants of Abraham. They were known as Israelites in the Old
Testament until they went into exile in Babylon. Then, from that
point forward, they were known as "Jews." Isaiah 5:2 calls them
the "choicest vine." They were blessed to be "adopted as sons."
Exodus 4:22 says, "Israel is my first born son." Exodus 19:6 tells
us that Israel is "a kingdom of priests and a holy nation." Hosea
11:1 says, "When Israel was a child, I loved him, and out of Egypt
I called **my son**."

In the Old Testament, God is referred to as the Father of
Israel, but not of individual Jews. However, the New Testament
refers to God, not only as the Father of Israel, but also as the Father
of individual believers. The Jewish leaders reacted with anger
against Jesus when he referred to God as His Father.

The Jews were blessed because God revealed to them "His
divine glory." The glory of God is the actual **presence** of God.
This goes all the way back to the Old Testament when He appeared
to the Israelites in the clouds (in Ex 24:16-17 at Mount Sinai, in
Ex. 16:10, and many other times).

They were blessed by the giving of the covenants. The first
covenant was given to Abraham (Genesis 12:15-17). Moses was

given a covenant (Exodus 19-31), as well as David (2 Samuel 7:8-16). We are also told it would be through Israel that God's supreme covenant, Jesus Christ, would manifest (Jeremiah 31:31-34 and Ezekiel 37:26).

Israel was blessed by the "giving of the Law." The Law included the Ten Commandments, as well as countless other principles and standards. In Romans 3:2, Paul told them that they had been the custodians of "the very words of God." They were blessed by being entrusted with the "temple service." This refers to the entire ceremonial system that God revealed to Moses, which would include the sacrifices, offerings, and cleansings performed by the Levites and priests.

Israel was blessed for they were given "the promises of God." Paul does not go into detail about the nature of these promises, but it seems that he is referring to the promise of the Messiah, Jesus Christ. Acts 2:39 says, "The promise is for you and all your children and for all who are far off – for all whom the Lord our God will call." Similarly, Acts 13:32-34 tells us, "We tell you the good news: What God promised our fathers he has fulfilled for us, their children, by raising up Jesus. As it is written in the second Psalm: 'You are my Son; today I have become your Father.'" The fact that God raised him from the dead, never to decay, is stated in these words: "I will give you the holy and sure blessings promised to David" (Acts 13:34).

They were blessed that God raised up through them "the fathers" of our faith and He allowed them to provide the lineage to the Savior of the world. It was no accident that Christ was born a Jew. He was preordained to be a human descendant of Abraham and David. The Book of Matthew shows the lineage of His father Joseph and the Book of Luke shows the genealogy of His natural mother, Mary. Jesus said that He was the promised Jewish Messiah who would offer salvation to all mankind (John 4:22-26).

"Theirs are the patriarchs, and from them is traced the human ancestry of Christ, who is God over all, forever praised. Amen!" (Romans 9:5). These words are an affirmation that Jesus

Christ is God. They affirm His majesty, His Lordship. Without exception, in both the Old and New Testaments, a doxology always places the word "blessed or praised" before the name of God. Here Paul used the reverse form, "God... forever praised," indicating that he intentionally equates Christ with God.

Just think of all the blessings God has given to us here in the United States and yet still people reject Him, His love, His mercy, His forgiveness. Think of ways you have been personally blessed by God. Write them out and post them on your mirror or somewhere at your job to remind you of the blessings of God in your life.

CHAPTER 39
ISRAEL'S UNBELIEF
Romans 9:30-33

"As it is written: 'See, I lay in Zion a stone that causes men to stumble and a rock that makes them fall, and the one who trusts in him will never be put to shame'."- Romans 9:33

In this chapter, Paul skillfully addresses the issue of the love of God for Israel and how it relates to Israel's unbelief. Paul's analysis of the problem of the Jewish people is clear and comprehensive. The first thing he does is tell them how he sees the problem. He begins the chapter telling them of the burden he bears because of their sinful ways. He even goes so far as to say that he wishes he could be accursed, or judged to hell, on their behalf. Then he lists nine privileges that God gave to Israel as His chosen people. The final privilege is that God brought the Savior into the world through them.

One of the most meaningful facts is that Christ came out of a Jewish bloodline. He was born of a Jewish mother and raised in a Hebrew home. He attended a Jewish synagogue and was given a Jewish education. He lived and labored in the promised land. Yet, in spite of all of these blessings and privileges, the Jews rejected Him. John 1:11 tells us, "He came to that which was his own, but his own did not receive him."

What does this say about God – did He and His word fail? This is the concern Paul addresses in Romans 9:6. In answering this question, he gives us four principles about God that he wants us to understand:

1) **The Principle of the Faithfulness of God** (vv. 6-13)

Verse 6: Paul asks if God's promise to Israel failed. In answer, he makes two points:

- God's election was not a matter of natural descent (vv. 6-10). He illustrates this by telling the story of the birth of Abraham's children. Abraham had children by two women, one of whom was his servant, Hagar. She bore a son named Ishmael, who became the father of the Arabs. Abraham's wife, Sarah, bore Isaac. Through Isaac came the Jewish nation. Isaac married a woman named Rebecca. They had twin boys, Esau and Jacob. Esau was born first; thus, he would become the rightful heir since he was the oldest. However, God chose Jacob for this honor instead. Paul's point here is this: God did not choose Jacob on the basis of physical natural descent. He is sovereign and He can do what He wants to do.

- God's Election is not based on human merit (vv.11-13). God chose Jacob before he and Esau were born. Neither had yet sinned; therefore God's choice was not based on human merit.

Verse 13: This passage quotes Malachi 1:2-3, which says, *"Jacob I loved, but Esau I hated."* This does not mean God hated the person of Esau; but Esau later became the father of the nation of Edom, which was very idolatrous and hated the Jews. God had promised to bless the Jewish people, but, because of their unbelief, they had lost His blessing. Israel's failure was their own and not God's. Paul shows that salvation is not and never has been based on heritage, merit, or lineage. Your parents or spouse being Christians does not automatically make you one. Paul is saying that salvation is based on God's promise and does not flow through lines of heredity. Rather, it flows through the lines of faith.

2) **The Principle of the Mercy of God** (vv. 14-18)

Verse 14: This verse raises another big question: "Is God unjust?" God chose one over the other.

Verse 15: *"For he says to Moses, 'I will have mercy on whom I have mercy, and I will have compassion on whom I have compassion.'"* This is a quote from Exodus 33:19. Paul is simply saying that God is sovereign and merciful.

Verses 16-18: Paul illustrates his point by telling about Pharaoh. God does not harden hearts directly. Hearts are hardened because people reject God over a period of time. A hard heart is the natural result of rejecting God. Our salvation is totally dependent on God's mercy! As sinners, we all deserve death.

3) The Principle of the Purpose of God (vv. 19-29)

This is a longer passage and involves a series of seven questions. Paul also quotes the Old Testament throughout this passage. Three main points in this passage are:

- Who are we to argue with God? (vv.19-21): God is the potter and we are the clay.

- God has His purposes (vv. 22-24): His ultimate purpose was to form His church from both Jews and Gentiles (v. 24).

- All of this was prophesied (vv. 25-29): He quotes: Hosea 2:23 in verse 25; Hosea 1:10 in verse 26; Isaiah 10:22-23 in verse 27; Isaiah 10:2-3 in verse 28; and Isaiah 1:9 in verse 29.

What does all of this mean? It means that the nation of Israel rejected God's purpose and plan to use them and glorify Him but this did not keep Him from keeping His word. Their denial did not defeat His purposes.

4) The Principle of the Grace of God (vv. 30-33)

In this passage Paul explains that the Jews sought righteousness by trying to keep the law. Yet, no one but Christ, in His perfection, was able to do that. Even though the Gentiles were not seeking righteousness, they still found it. When the Gentiles heard the message, thousands responded.

Verse 33: *"As it is written: 'See, I lay in Zion a stone that causes men to stumble and a rock that makes them fall, and the one who trusts in him will never be put to shame.'"* Paul's final Old Testament quotation is from Isaiah 28:16. The stone here is Christ, God's Stone of Salvation.

It is not God's will that anyone should perish. He offers salvation to "whoever wishes" (Revelations 22:17). God has given man a free will. We have the choice to reject Christ or receive Christ as our own personal Lord and Savior.

CHAPTER 40
HOW TO GET THE REAL DEAL
Romans 10:1-10

"Christ is the end of the law so that there may be righteousness for everyone who believes."- Romans 10:4

A person's walk of faith starts with the free gift of salvation from God, which transforms over time into a deep, personal relationship with Christ. Apart from Christ, one can never receive the gift of being declared righteous. In other words, there is only one way to be put right with God and that is by way of faith in Christ. Paul mentions the Jews in verses 1-3. In verse 1, he states that it is his *"desire and prayer to God to see all Jews be saved."* If this was Paul's desire, what should our desire be? The same.

Verse 2: *"For I can testify about them that they are zealous for God but their zeal is not based on knowledge."* Paul knew the Jews very well before his conversion because he himself was a zealous Jew. So, in these verses Paul is speaking from a position of understanding.

Verse 3: *"Since they did not know the righteousness that comes from God, and sought to establish their own, they did not submit to God's righteousness."* Paul is saying that in their failure to understand the righteousness of Christ, they also refused to submit themselves to the authority of Christ. **Before we can understand the righteousness of Christ, we must submit ourselves under the authority of Christ.** We must know the righteousness that comes from God. We have talked in past chapters about the exchange of man's sins for the righteousness of Christ. When we are declared not guilty, we are **"justified"** at that very moment. When we are made righteous in Christ and we stand before God we are given the privileges and the inheritance of Christ.

Verse 4: *"Christ is the end of the Law so that there may be righteousness for everyone who believes."* The Jews lived their lives based on tradition and customs in addition to God's Law to try to make themselves acceptable in God's sight. Here's the whole point: Our human efforts cannot substitute for the righteousness of God. We can only substitute God's righteousness with the Law if we are perfect; but since no one is perfect, we cannot do enough on our own to become righteous. In faith we are made righteous in Christ. The Law ends in Christ. This means that Christ fulfilled the purpose and the goal of the Law, which is to point people to God. The Law shows us how bad off we are without Christ.

Verse 5: *"Moses describes in this way the righteousness that is by the Law, 'The man who does these things will live by them.'"* Why did God give the Law when He knew people could not keep the Law? Galatians 3:24-25 says, "So the Law was put in charge to lead us to Christ that we might be justified by faith. Now that faith has come we are no longer under the supervisions of the Law." The Law teaches us that we need salvation in Christ. God's grace gives us that salvation. Does the Old Testament apply? Yes, because in it God reveals His nature, His humanity, His moral laws, and His guidelines for living. But we cannot be saved only by keeping the Law. We must trust in Christ. God's salvation is here today. All that's required of us is to respond to His free gift of salvation.

The next verse is the key to this chapter. Verse 9: *"If you confess with your mouth, 'Jesus is Lord,' and believe in your heart that God raised Him from the dead, you will be saved."* Paul outlines the process a person must take to receive the free gift of salvation. To confess with your mouth in a public setting enables a person to show his true love for Christ. When a person gets married they must have a witness - in a way, make a public declaration. Why? So that everyone will know. We cannot be ashamed of Christ and live for Him at the same time. Paul says we must also believe in our hearts that God raised Christ from the dead. In other words, put our faith and trust in the fact that God is real and Christ is real and dedicate our life to His leadership.

When we accept Christ in faith, what does that mean? What is faith? Faith is the foundation of the Christian life. Faith is having a hope in something one hasn't seen. If we could see the object of our faith it would not be true faith. 2 Corinthians 5:7 teaches us to **"walk by faith, not by sight."** In a strange way, our faith is all of who we are that is significant in God's eyes. 1 Peter 1:3-10 says that God gives us the power we need to live a godly life. He gives us faith and wants to reproduce His character in us through the righteousness of Christ. God demands our discipline and our efforts.

As we follow Christ, the Holy Spirit guides us and we develop self-control, patience, and faith. Faith is beyond what we believe. Our faith must become an integrated, dynamic part of everything we do. Without Christ's guidance, men have weak faith. Weak faith is an immature faith that lacks muscle to stand against external pressures. Paul says in Romans 3:28, "For we maintain that man is justified in faith." Why does God save us by faith alone? There are several reasons for this:

1) Faith eliminates pride and human effort. Man must be stripped of his pride to place his trust in Christ.

2) Faith exalts what God has done and not what people do.

3) Faith admits that we need help and that we are sinners who will never measure up.

4) Faith is based on our relationship with God and not our performance for God.

CHAPTER 41
WHAT DOES IT TAKE TO BE SAVED?
Romans 10:11-21

*"How, then, can they call on the one they have not believed in?
And how can they believe in the one of whom they have not heard?
And how can they hear without someone preaching to them?"*
- Romans 10:14

In the first ten verses of this chapter Paul shared with us about Israel's rejection of the Messiah. First, Paul told us that they were ignorant of the provision of Christ (v. 4a). In other words, those who think that they are already righteous due to their own good life and works are actually ignorant. Secondly, Israel was ignorant that faith and not works is the basis of salvation (vv. 4b-10). Paul explains clearly what one must do to be saved in verse 9. Salvation has two parts:

1) **God's Part:** He offers the gospel and eternal life.

2) **Man's Part:** We must respond by repenting of our sins, confessing Jesus as our Lord, and surrendering our life to Him. There is no such thing in the Bible as accepting Christ as our Savior and not our Lord.

The Jews strongly rejected the idea that God's grace extended to the Gentiles. In spite of the prophets preaching this theme throughout the Old Testament, they chose not to listen. Thus, the end result was that they also rejected Christ as their Messiah.

Verse 11: *"The Scripture says, 'Whoever believes in Him will not be disappointed.'"* Paul is quoting Isaiah 28:16 and saying that God has always been calling the Gentiles. The barrier to salvation is not racial or cultural. It is the choice of man to reject God and His revelation. This is true even in modern Israel, where most of the Jews oppose Christian missionary work and are strongly opposed to Christianity. Acts 21:28 talks about how they view the Christian faith as against their people and the Law.

Verse 12: *"No distinction between the Jew and the Greek; for the same Lord is Lord of all, abounding in riches for all who call upon Him."* There are not two or more gods or multiple ways of salvation. Christ is the only way. This angers many people and they call Christians intolerant. However, one must understand why this is true. There is one and only one payment for sin that God will accept. Romans 6:23 tells us clearly that either we will die for our sins or someone else will die in our place. The gospel is that Christ died for us. He was a human sacrifice in our place and he shed his blood to pay for our sins. The one who died for us had to live a perfect life without sin and fulfill all the Law. The only one that could do that would be God Himself. So, God became a man, born of a virgin, lived a perfect life, died on a cross, and shed His blood to the debt of your sins in your place. Then He rose again and He is alive right now and wants to live in your heart. That is the gospel. No other religion in the world has a Savior. No other religion in the world offers a sinless human sacrifice for sins other than Jesus Christ. So, God has made Jesus our one and only Lord. One of the biggest threats today in the modern church is universalism, which says that Jesus is "a" way but not necessarily "the" way.

Verse 13: *"Whoever calls on the name of the Lord will be saved."* This is a quote from Joel 2:32. God offers salvation in Christ and one must choose to receive or reject Christ. Notice it says "Lord" here. We must confess that Jesus is the Lord, Creator God and He will be the Ruler and Master of our life. Think of salvation as a Kingdom. There can only be one King. Salvation takes place when we decide to step off of the throne and allow Jesus to be our King, our Lord. False salvation is when one just wants to use Christ as a fire insurance salesman to not go to hell with no intention of allowing Christ to change one's life and rule over one's heart. Notice the word "saved" here. Many do not like to use this term today; however, it is used in the Old Testament 160 times. It is used in the New Testament over 100 times. Paul himself uses it 45 times. It simply means "to be made whole."

Verses 14-15: Paul asks four rhetorical questions in order to demonstrate the necessity of evangelism. Read all four questions. Then read them backwards from last to first.

1) How can one call if he does not believe?

2) How can one believe if he has not heard?

3) How can one hear without a preacher?

4) How can they preach unless they are sent?

Paul tells us that it is not the physical feet that are beautiful but the wonderful glad tidings that those feet carry to the ends of the earth.

Verses 16-21: In these verses Paul quotes the Old Testament five times. He explains that Israel heard the Word of the Lord but chose to reject it. Man has a choice to reject or receive Christ. Ask yourself this question: Am I like Israel, a person who is disobedient and obstinate (v. 21)? If you are lost, you can call on Christ to be your Lord and Savior today. If we know Him as Lord then it is our responsibility to share our faith with those who do not. Look at those four questions and apply them to your life.

CHAPTER 42
GOD WILL KEEP HIS PROMISE TO ISRAEL
Romans 11:1-10

"At the present time there is a remnant chosen by grace."
- Romans 11:5

Verse 1: *"I ask then: Did God reject his people? By no means! I am an Israelite myself, a descendant of Abraham, from the tribe of Benjamin."* Paul also shows us that not all Jews have rejected Christ. *"God did not reject his people, whom he foreknew. Don't you know what the Scripture says in the passage about Elijah—how he appealed to God against Israel."* Paul wanted so badly for his people, the Jews, to accept Christ in faith, but, in verse 5, he quotes Isaiah 1:9, *"Only the remnant will be saved."* In other words, God has already laid out the fact that only a few Jews would accept Christ. Let me ask you a question: Did that keep Paul from preaching the Gospel? No.

Let's go to Verse 6: *"And if by grace, then it is no longer works; if it were, grace would no longer be grace."* Do you think it's easier for God to love you when you're good? Do you think some people are so bad they can't possibly be saved? If one thinks this way, one does not fully understand that salvation is by grace, which means it's a free gift; it cannot be earned. It can only be accepted with thankfulness and praise. Do you ever wonder if your faith is strong enough to save you? Again, to think this way is to completely miss the point. **It's Christ who saves us, not our feelings, not our actions, but His strength, which is "mighty to save."** Jesus Christ offers us salvation, not because of what we do, but because of His unconditional love for all mankind. What is the rule of faith? **Faith is the knowledge that we are weak and the belief that He is strong**. Faith is simply when we reach out to Christ and accept His free gift of eternal life.

Verse 7: *"What then? What has Israel sought to earn that it did not obtain, but the elect did? The others were hardened."*

Romans 9:31-32 says, "But Israel, who pursued a law of righteousness, has not obtained it. Why not? Because they pursued it, not by faith, but as if it were, by works." This is a tough pill to swallow. Oftentimes we are like the Israelites. We try to get right with **God by attending church, going to Bible studies, being nice to people.** After all, we've played by the rules, haven't we? Paul clearly tells us that this approach never succeeds. God's plan for us is not for us to try to earn His favor, because we will never be good enough. Therefore, we must simply put our trust in Him. Christ will set us free with His grace when we put our faith in Him. If we do that, He will never let us down.

Who is the stumbling stone? Christ. The Jews could not believe in Him because He did not meet their expectations. Even today, people stumble over Christ. When our values are opposite of Christ, we will stumble. Jesus wants us to come humbly before Him, but many are afraid to humble themselves as a child in His presence. Let me ask you a question: What in your life is causing you to stumble over Jesus? **Many of us are works driven. We must understand that our salvation in Christ is not tied to how much we do for God.** We are saved by grace in faith alone. Verse 7 describes how God removed the Jews' ability to see the world as it is.

God's Word is powerful. When we look at God's Word, we should ask three questions:

1) What did it mean then?
2) How does it apply now?
3) How does it apply to my life?

The Word of God should be to our spirit as blood is to the body. He who angers us, controls us. God doesn't want me to do something for Him; He wants to do something through me. **One's spiritual life will not be any deeper than one's devotional life.** Ask yourself: Am I living my life in a way that is worth Christ dying for?

CHAPTER 43

UNIFICATION OF THE CHURCH
Romans 11:11-24

"As far as the gospel is concerned, they are enemies on your account; but as far as election is concerned, they are loved on account of the patriarchs."- Romans 11:28

This chapter offers us a close look at the passion Paul has for the unification of the church. He had a vision of the church in which both Jews and Gentiles united together in the love of God and obedience to Christ. Paul visualized this church looking to Christ alone for salvation. He believed that a person's ethnic background and social standing were not relevant to a person's spiritual standing. What really mattered was their faith in Christ.

Turn to Galatians 3:26-29. "You are all sons of God through faith in Christ Jesus, for all of you who were baptized into Christ have clothed yourselves with Christ. There is neither Jew nor Greek, slave nor free, male nor female, for you are all one in Christ Jesus. If you belong to Christ, then you are Abraham's seed, and heirs according to the promise." In Roman society, a young man coming of age literally laid aside the robe of childhood and put on a new toga. This symbolized his move into adult citizenship, with full rights and responsibilities. In these verses, Paul combines this cultural understanding of growth with the concept of baptism. He is saying that by becoming a believer in Christ and being baptized into Christ, we have clothed ourselves with Christ. When we are baptized with Christ, we become one in Christ. **To clothe our self with Christ means to lay down our old way of living and mature into a new life in Christ.**

Verses 28: *"There is neither Jew nor Greek, slave nor free, male nor female, for you are all one in Christ Jesus."* This verse hits us right between the eyes. There's not one of us that is any better than anyone else. Here's the crazy part, though: Some of us believe we are better than someone else. In Christ, we are all joint

185

heirs with Him. We must ask ourselves which we would rather be: rich on earth and poor in heaven, or poor on earth and rich in heaven. **What we respect we will attract.** Many Jews would wake up in the morning and pray, "Lord, thank You for not making me a Gentile." White guys, it would be like you praying, "Lord, thank you for not making me black."

Faith in Christ transcends all difficulties and puts us all together on level ground at the foot of the cross. Just because we are different does not mean we can't associate with others outside our comfort zone. **All men see color.** There's not one person reading this book that can fully separate himself from a racial divide; but Christ does not see color. So, if Christ does not see color, and Christ lives in us, we too, in Christ, can become color blind. It's not our power that enables us to see through all the prejudices, but the power in Christ that lives in us.

Go to Ephesians 2:14, "For He Himself is our peace." Christ is the ultimate unifier with people. Christ destroys the barriers between people. He removes the walls so that different races can enjoy unity together. When Christ died on the cross, all of the anger between races died with Him. Unfortunately, many times Christians fail to allow Christ to permeate every part of their lives. Jesus accepted people where they were regardless of who they were, as long as they simply committed to following Him. Can we be the light of the world and hide out with other Christians, isolated from the hunger and poverty of the real world? I don't think so. God has called us to be the hands and feet of Jesus. If we create fancy Christian country clubs, are we any better than the Pharisees? Jesus came to bust up the club. His package is all-inclusive, available to both Jews and Gentiles, alike. Christ died for us, so our anger and resentment must die with Him. He arose from the grave and so does our new life in Him. If you are alive, God has a plan for your life. The first step for all of us is to ask God to show us ourselves for what we really are. Think about this: **You cannot confess to God what you can't admit to yourself.**

CHAPTER 44

CHRIST + *I AM NOTHING* = CHRISTIAN
Romans 11:25-32

"Just as you who were at one time disobedient to God have now received mercy as a result of their disobedience."-
Romans 11:30

This chapter deals with the abundance of love God has for His chosen people, Israel. God clearly loves two major entities in the Bible: Israel and the church. Paul shows us how God will save Israel as a nation and how there will be people of Israel saved because of God's promise to His people. Turn to Deuteronomy 7:6: "For you are a people holy to the Lord your God. The Lord your God has chosen you out of all the peoples on the face of the Earth to be His people, His treasured possession." Just like God chose Israel, God chose us. God did not come to us because we are deserving. Instead, God chose us out of His love and grace. At the end of the day we must understand the equation for a Christian: **Christ + I Am Nothing = Christian**. In order for us to truly follow Christ, we must empty ourselves to become "nothing." Anything else we put in the equation equals something other than a true Christian.

The concept of humility began early in the Old Testament. Deuteronomy 8:2-3, **"Remember how the LORD your God led you all the way in the wilderness these forty years, to humble and test you in order to know what was in your heart, whether or not you would keep his commands. He humbled you, causing you to hunger and then feeding you with manna, which neither you nor your ancestors had known, to teach you that man does not live on bread alone but on every word that comes from the mouth of the LORD."** Before we can become "nothing" we must be humbled. Pride is the opposite of humility. Proverbs 16:18 says, "Pride goes before destruction." The crazy thing about proud people is that they cannot see pride in themselves, but most everyone else recognizes it. Proverbs 13:10, **"Pride only breeds** quarrels." A proud person is never wrong and always right, and most of the time *has* to be right. **To admit that one is wrong requires a sense of humility and is a sign of inner strength and of maturity in Christ.** It takes a secure, loving person to admit their mistakes. These are the teachings of Christ. To always see faults in others and not ourselves keeps us from ever dealing with who we really are.

In this passage, Paul shows how the Jews and the Gentiles benefit from each other. Whenever one group receives mercy from God, the other group shares in the blessings. In God's original plan, Jesus would be the source of God's blessing to the Gentile (Genesis 12:3). When the Jews rejected the mission, God blessed the Gentiles anyway through the Jewish Messiah, Jesus. He still maintained His love for the Jews because of His promise to them. God is looking for the day that both Gentiles and Jews will be humbled and drawn together for His glory.

In order to become nothing, we must receive God's forgiveness, we must forgive ourselves and then we must forgive others (Matthew 6:14-15). We will be forgiven to the extent that we can forgive others. **If I refuse to forgive others, God will refuse to forgive me.** I am convinced of something that I believe to be true: Most people have someone in their life they have not fully forgiven. Is it easier to ask God for forgiveness or grant forgiveness to someone else? Before we ask God to forgive us, we must ask ourselves if we have forgiven others who have wronged us. Our ability to forgive others becomes a measuring stick of our maturity in the Lord. We forgive because Christ forgave us first. **Hurt people, hurt people.** People who hold grudges and cannot admit their wrongs ultimately end up not forgiving people, which ends up hurting people. Before we can become "I am nothing," we must have a forgiving heart. One of the hardest things to do is to humbly forgive others. Growth requires faith. It's not about having great faith, but it's about having faith in a great God. Let me close with this: **The greatest need a person has is to discover that God is all he needs.**

CHAPTER 45
JUST HOLD ON, HELP IS ON THE WAY
Romans 11:33-36

"Oh, the depth of the riches of the wisdom and knowledge of God! How unsearchable his judgments, and his paths beyond tracing out!"- Romans 11:33

This chapter opens up the door to many unanswered questions many of us have today. The implication of verses 33-36 is that each question helps us realize that no one has fully understood the mind of God. No one has ever counseled God. God owes us nothing. We can agree that following Jesus can be difficult and it's hard for us to totally and fully understand the ways of God. As a matter of fact, Paul asks us in verse 34, *"Who has known the mind of the Lord? Or who has been his counselor?"* God is incomprehensible and we will never know Him completely, but we can have knowledge about God, which is given to us through His Word. The Bible is full of details about who God is, how we can know Him, and how we can have an eternal relationship with Him; but at the end of the day, we can never know enough to answer all of life's questions.

We cannot manipulate God. The bottom line is that life creates more questions than answers. These questions force us to either come to God humbly in faith requesting a fresh new insight or try to put our own self will to action, which usually ends in frustration and destruction. Men, the hardest thing we have to do is to get out of our own way of doing things. What Paul is really asking us in verse 35 is, "Who has ever given to God, that God should repay him?" **There's nothing we have that God needs.** We must come to a point in our lives where we start to truly, wholeheartedly believe that we are nothing without God. Paul tells us in this passage that nothing compares to God. His power, His grace, His mercy, and His love are so much more than we can comprehend. Look at verse 36: *"For from him and through him and to him are all things. To him be the glory forever! Amen."* If we look at Job's life, we see Job's friends had a whole lot of answers for Job. They saw the bad things in Job's life and associated these things with sin in his life, and they were hard on Job for his perceived lack of obedience. We are in need of God. All good things are connected to God.

Many of you are giving up hope because God has been silent and you are getting discouraged. Don't give up. Don't lose hope. There's an old spiritual that says, **"Just hold on 'cause help is on the way."** God will speak. Be patient. Most of all be respectful. Whatever you love you will respect. Whatever you respect you will love. God can speak to us in many ways:

1) **Through His Word:** God's Word is powerful and when we come to it with an open heart and mind, God can change us into who He wants us to be.

2) **Through Prayer:** When you pray, ask God to reveal things to you that are in accordance with His will.

3) **Through the Holy Spirit:** The Spirit of God will encourage us with strength, faith, and courage to do things that are not natural to us or to the world. Most of what God wants us to do is not natural in our world to do.

4) **Through relationships:** Christ-following family members, close friends, and spouses can help point us in the right direction.

In Job 38:1-2, God answers Job's questions with His own questions. God used Job's ignorance of the earth's natural order to reveal Job's ignorance of God's moral and spiritual order. God was showing him that if he could not understand the science behind the physical laws of the universe, how could he ever understand the spiritual laws of the universe? If God is the standard and we admit we are nothing, then our only option is to submit to His authority and rest in His care. God has all the forces of nature at His command. **Whatever God does is fair, whether we understand it or not**. His will is perfect. He uses His power according to His perfection. Our power is useless, but our humility gives us the power of the Lord. The smarter we are, the harder it is to truly trust in the Lord. Why? Because it's easy to draw on our own perceived strength. Sometimes a person who has material possessions or is highly intellectual does not really feel that he needs Jesus. God wants to reveal His greater purposes to you, but He will not reveal everything to you because it is too tough to live by our sight. **He wants us to live by faith.** Remember, with God's help the task ahead of us is never greater than the power behind us.

CHAPTER 46
LIVING SACRIFICE
Romans 12:1

"Therefore, I urge you, brothers, in view of God's mercy, to offer your bodies as living sacrifices, holy and pleasing to God—this is your spiritual act of worship."- Romans 12:1

Over the last few chapters we have studied the profound teachings of Paul regarding the tools God has instilled in us as believers. In this chapter, Paul now charges us believers with how we need to use those tools to live a life of peace. Have you ever asked yourself the question, "How do I live out the Christian life?" Do you always feel like you're coming up short? Do you always seem to struggle? Do you try hard but always seem to fail? Do you always feel discouraged? I want you to consider saying and making the following commitment. **"Today I will stop performing and I will start trusting more."**

Many well-intentioned Christians flock to seminars, churches, conferences, and Bible studies with the main theme of getting back on track, or "trying to perform better." I've got news for you: It doesn't work. You will never be able to try hard enough. The key to a productive and satisfying life as a Christian is not to try harder. It's to simply **"start trusting God more."** In this chapter we will just cover the first verse. There's a lot of meat on this bone so let's get started.

Let's read verse 1: *"Therefore, I urge you, brothers, in view of God's mercy, to offer your bodies as living sacrifices, holy and pleasing to God – this is your spiritual act of worship."* In the Old Testament, animals were sacrificed for the sins of the people. A priest would kill the animal, cut it into pieces and place it on the altar. But even in the Old Testament, God made it clear that obedience from the heart was more important than a sacrifice. Here in verse 1 Paul wants us to offer ourselves, not animals, as living sacrifices. **Here is a spiritual principle: God gave of Himself so that we might give of ourselves to Him.**

Let's go to Philippians 3:3: "We who worship by the Spirit of God, who glory in Christ, and who put no confidence in the flesh." Whatever we do, we cannot judge other's spirituality by their fulfillment of Christian duties or by their level of human activity. And don't think that we can ever satisfy God by how hard we work. God notices all we do for Him and will reward us for it, but only if our actions come from a loving heart that reflects the free gift of salvation. What Paul is talking about here is the difference between a person's soul and his body. A person's soul is what is redeemed when he is born again, but his body remains unredeemed (Romans 7:22-32). This verse says that the redeemed soul must reside in a body of flesh, which is still a magnet of sin. "To be redeemed" means "to be purchased." In other words, God bought us with His Son, Jesus Christ. Guess what? **We don't own ourselves.** When you came to Christ, you gave up all rights to yourself and became, as Paul puts it, "a slave to Christ." Who do slaves follow? Their owners. Men, this is a difficult position for us to put ourselves in because we always want to be in charge. But Christ is our ultimate authority. God owns us, so He wants to lead us with His Spirit to accomplish His will and His purpose.

The body by nature is a place of unholy thoughts and actions. By nature it is the center of sinful desires, emotional depression, spiritual doubts, and lack of faith. When we come to Christ in faith our soul is taken over by Christ and it is up to us to relinquish ourselves over to Christ so He can take over our bodies. In order for God to work through us, He must work through our bodies. Our souls will be controlled either by our spirit or by our flesh, which is our body. In other words, God has purchased my soul. It's redeemed. God transformed my soul by exchanging my sins for His righteousness, which means redemption, but my body is unredeemed until I get to heaven. Therefore, since my body is open or exposed to the world, it naturally gravitates toward sin.

Have you ever wondered why we can't live the perfect life as Christians? Because we have unredeemed bodies. Paul says, "I do the things I don't want to do" (Romans 7:15). Now, pay close attention. **We cannot totally keep sin out of our lives, but with the power of God we can keep sin from ruling our bodies.** You see, sin cannot reign in our souls because Christ already resides in the soul of a saved man. Sin will not reign in our bodies if, by the Spirit, we put to death the deeds of the body (Romans 8:11).

Let me explain. We must become nothing so that Christ can become everything in us. We must decrease so He can increase (John 3:30). We must die daily and take up our cross so that we can allow Him to live or take residence in our soul. (Luke 9:23) If He lives on the inside, He can express Himself through our body. The most supreme act of spiritual worship is to present ourselves as living sacrifices. You could say to me, "Why would God want me to give up myself as a living sacrifice?" Because that's exactly what He did for you and me. He gave His Son as a living sacrifice and He died so that we could be set free from the bondage of sin.

You do not own you. 1 Corinthians 6:19 says, "Our bodies belong to God." A person who wants to do what he wants is enslaved by his own desires. When the Holy Spirit comes into our lives and transforms us into the likeness of Christ our old self doesn't exist in us anymore. Our old self just got kicked out and the real owner just moved into His new home. Now, since He lives in us, and our old self doesn't live there anymore, He actually bought us for a price. What did it cost? It cost our life. Because we belong to God, we must operate under His standards and not our own. When we offer ourselves as a living sacrifice, we express the fullness of worship to God. Worship cannot be just a weekly event. **Worship must be a daily way of life.** Will you embrace the will of the Lord and ask Him to give you the strength to become a living sacrifice?

CHAPTER 47
LIVING SACRIFICES: Give Your Mind to God
Romans 12:2

"Do not conform any longer to the pattern of this world, but be transformed by the renewing of your mind. Then you will be able to test and approve what God's will is—his good, pleasing and perfect will."- Romans 12:2

This chapter comes on the heels of one of the greatest verses in the Bible. In the last chapter we read Romans 12:1: **"To present yourself as a living sacrifice."** Let's review. The goal of the last chapter was to not try harder, but to trust more. To present ourselves as living sacrifices requires us to offer all of our self, while realizing that we are nothing. We discussed that we don't own ourselves. We are redeemed by the death of Christ on the cross. Now we will look a little deeper into the **"how to."** In other words, how to "offer yourself as a living sacrifice unto God." What must we do? The first step is to give our mind to God.

Verse 2a: *"Do not be conformed to the world."* Before we can fully grasp this concept, we must understand what Paul is really trying to communicate in this verse. First, we need to know that there are primarily two types of forces that exist in the world. The first is the supernatural Spirit of God at work in the world. God uses His Spirit to work through people to accomplish His will and His work for His overall plan. John 14:16 says, "And I will ask the Father, and he will give you another Counselor to be with you forever." The job of the Holy Spirit is to assist and enable us each day, guiding and directing us in our decisions and in our spiritual development. The Holy Spirit is a being. It has emotions, intellect, and a will. The Holy Spirit is a person. The Holy Spirit is part of the Trinity – God the Father, God the Son, and God the Holy Spirit – three distinct beings operating in the same direction, but all one in the same.

Second, there are evil forces. Evil forces come from Satan. Genesis 3:17 say, "To Adam he said, 'Because you listened to your wife and ate from the tree about which I commanded you, 'You must not eat of it.' Cursed is the ground because of you; through painful toil you will eat of it all the days of your life." Because of the fall of mankind, humans are naturally depraved. We are infected with a disease called sin. The evil spirit of sin is born into the body of man. All people have this problem with sin. The human tendency is to allow the world to conform us.

But Paul tells us here, "Do not be conformed to this world." As Christians, we are set free from the bondage of sin. The word "**conform**" in the Greek means, **"putting on an act."** In other words, we should not allow ourselves to try to be like or put on an act to impress someone else while conforming to the world. The reverse is also true. We are to not put on an act trying to be holier than we are and all self-righteous. God wants us to simply be ourselves, but allow Christ to express Himself through us. You see this is the key part of the lesson. This is the part I want to make sure you clearly understand. When Christ comes into our life, our inner man is filled with the Holy Spirit (Romans 8:9). The Holy Spirit is the agent of change in our life.

So, if the Holy Spirit is the only way to accomplish an outward change, it must come from the filling of the Spirit of God. When we get saved, we have the capacity to have a connection with the Lord. Once we are saved, we are given the power of the Spirit. **God is the source of all power.** Therefore, when Paul says not "to be conformed to this world," he is instructing us to allow the Holy Spirit of God to lead us into His world, not the world that **"that Satan rules."** We cannot do what the world does and also present our self as a living sacrifice. As we discussed in the last chapter, sin will enter our lives, but as Christians we must let the Holy Spirit lead our lives so that sin does not rule in us.

The next part is a strong case for God's Word instructing us. Verse 2a: *"But be transformed by the renewing of your mind."* The Holy Spirit achieves this transformation by a renewing of the mind. David testified in Psalms 119:11, "Thy Word I have treasured in my heart that I may not sin against Thee." The renewing process comes from when we seek the Lord in His Word and the Holy Spirit in turn renews our mind. Colossians 3:16 says, "Let the Word of Christ dwell in us with all wisdom and teaching." Colossians 3:2 says, "It is the mind set on the things above, not on the things of the earth." This kind of mind is the only mind that can present itself as a living sacrifice.

Verse 2b: *"That you may prove what the will of God is, that it is good and acceptable and perfect."* Paul is really saying that when a believer's mind is transformed, his thinking, moral reasoning, and spiritual understanding are able to properly evaluate everything and accept what conforms to the will of God. Here's the deal: Most of us set ourselves up to fail when it comes to God's standards. We say to ourselves, "I deserve this new house. I've worked hard. It's my money. It's my life and I can do what I want to do." You see this is a "fleshly" attitude, meaning our sinful flesh is in control. The other option is to say to ourselves, "How can I honor God in this situation?

The other option is to say to ourselves "How can I seek the will of God in this situation?" By doing this we prove that the will of God is that which is good and acceptable and perfect to Him. The concept of the will of God is this: We must dedicate our lives to submitting to God **to do exactly what God would have us do**. This is a key part for us to understand. When our mind is transformed, our will to do what God wants us to do will be transformed. The product of a transformed mind is a life that is obedient to God. I have to confess, I'm not there yet. I am still a work in progress. God continues to renew and transform me. The hardest thing for me to do is to die to my old self. When our self becomes the most important part of the equation, we fall out of fellowship with the Lord.

What hurts us when we are out of fellowship with the Lord? Galatians 5:17 says, "The flesh lost against the spirit." In other words, flesh makes self the center and elevates **self-will** above **God's will**. We may serve God, but it's how we want to serve Him, not the way that He wants us to serve Him. **Self-will**

always does good in its own eyes. Self is the principle behind every action. Self never fails to want its way even at the expense of allowing the flesh to take over. Self always opposes the Holy Spirit.

Self always wants its way. **Self admires righteousness.** Therefore, self always tries to act righteous. Self has not learned to hate the **"old self."** Self does not want to be liberated from sin. Self wants to always look good externally. Self wants to be noticed, but self does not see the real problem. Self feeds on itself. **The problem is that self can never be controlled.** It's like a wild dog with rabies. It must be destroyed. You see, self is our greatest problem. Self believes it can become righteous by doing good. When self is in control, self promotes self. For this very reason self must die - not your physical self, but the selfish part of you.

Romans 8:8 says, "Those who are in the flesh cannot please God." You see, "we are saved by grace through faith in the Lord" (Ephesians 2:8), so God does the saving, not us. Therefore, we cannot become more righteous through "self" trying to be righteous. **Self must be destroyed. Self must be crucified. Self must die. We must die to self before we can truly live an abundant life in Christ.** We must die so that Christ can be resurrected in our new life and live in us. When self is crucified, pride also dies. Bitterness also dies. Hatred dies, loneliness dies, all evilness dies and God graces us by a pouring out of the unconditional love of Christ. This love binds all things together for the glory of God. It looks beyond self. It puts others before itself. This love is kind and loves even those who cannot give love back. A death must occur before abundant life can be received.

The only way the *agape* love of God can be in our life is to **destroy self**. Most of the time one must be at a breaking point to realize self is the problem. As long as everything is going great, most people see themselves in a "great light" in comparison to everyone else. But when self hits the bottom, self can start the climb back by beginning to give up the "old ways" and living a life of faith in God, covered by His grace. God's grace is so great. It's so awesome that we will be given grace 24 hours a day, 365 days a year for eternity. Why can't we let "self" die so that Christ can truly live? I'm still working on this myself. I do realize now that it's **"not I, but Christ."** This concept will set you free from all the underlying issues of your life. Your life is not about you; it's all about allowing Christ to deliver you from your sin with His power, His mercy, and His grace.

CHAPTER 48
LIVING SACRIFICES:
The Attitude of True Humility
Romans 12:3-8

"For by the grace given me I say to every one of you: Do not think of yourself more highly than you ought, but rather think of yourself with sober judgment, in accordance with the measure of faith God has given you."- Romans 12:3

The last two chapters address issues that are at the heart of living the Christian life. Paul tells us in 12:1 that the most important display of worship is expressed when we offer our bodies as a living sacrifice. As we discussed before, there is a fundamental concept here that is critical for us to understand. When we are saved, our soul belongs to God because it is redeemed. So in effect, God owns us or, He owns our inner person.

You see, we have an inner person, the soul, which is led by the Spirit, and we have an outer person, which is our body. Our body, the outer man, follows whatever dominates our soul. Our soul is dominated either by "self" or by the "Spirit." When we present our self or our body as a living sacrifice, we are giving up of ourselves to God. We are putting our bodies to death so that Christ may live in us. The person keeping us away from living an abundant life in Christ is our self, not anyone else. We struggle with most issues because of our lack of confidence in the Holy Spirit. We doubt God's will for our lives. The object of our body is to please itself. Who are we direct descendants of? Adam. What problem did Adam create for us? He gave into the temptation of sin; therefore, we have the same problem. Everyone has this problem.

Let's go back to Romans 6:11: *"Count yourselves dead to sin but alive to God in Christ Jesus."* Will you consider allowing God to transform you into what He wants you to become? The first step is to destroy "self." Self does not desire to follow Christ. Self does not want to be sold out to the Lord. Self wants to be in control at all times. Self loves attention. Self seeks pleasure. To follow Christ means to deny everything that originates within us. To follow Christ means to deny what we have, what we can do, and realize that we are nothing without Him. Paul said **"not I but Christ."** Our focus should not be on ourselves, but on Christ. **To deny self is to live in Christ.**

In this chapter, Paul says in verse 3, *"Do not think of yourself more highly than you ought."* Having a balanced view of our self is important. Some of us think of ourselves too highly and some of us feel sorry for our self. Both are wrong attitudes. Most of us tie ourselves to what other people think, but our true value is in what God thinks. Pride is a direct result of "self." If pride exists in our life or our life is filled with pride, it's hard to produce eternal results. The most common attitude of human nature is pride. Those of you thinking, "I don't have any pride" – you're the very one who is eaten up with pride. Those of you who would say, "I am a proud person" – you are on the first step to humility. To understand how pride affects our walk with the Lord is to move to humility. Without humility, the Holy Spirit cannot exist in us. Paul speaks of this type of humble love in 1 Corinthians 13.

Let's go to 1 Peter 5:5-7: "Clothe yourselves with humility toward one another, for God is opposed to the proud, but gives grace to the humble. Humble yourselves, therefore, under God's mighty hand. Cast all your anxiety on Him because He cares for you." It takes a humble person to admit they have a problem. It takes a person absent of all pride to follow instructions of an older, wiser person. It takes a humble person to obey God. It takes a humble person to confess their wrongs before they are caught. It takes a humble person to seek the leadership of the Holy Spirit. When humility is present, the Holy Spirit is present. There are five wrong attitudes related to humility:

1) Boasting of our accomplishments or of our spiritual gifts. If we ever have to tell others about what we've done, or tell

others about our spiritual gifts, we're displaying a prideful spirit.

2) Depreciating our self is false humility (1 Corinthians 12:11-12). This is a poorly designed effort to receive praise from others.

3) To claim and talk about a supernatural spiritual gift, which makes you feel better about yourself, is a clear sign of a wrong attitude of humility.

4) To deny others of their spiritual gifts is a wrong attitude to have.

5) To fail to use our own gifts is also a wrong attitude.

CHAPTER 49
LOVE: THE KEY TO A CHRISTIAN LIFE
Romans 12:9-13

"Be devoted to one another in brotherly love. Honor one another above yourselves."- Romans 12:10

Our society is preoccupied with all types of activities to keep us focused on things that satisfy and entertain us to an extreme level. Sports, recreation, Hollywood, and music all have celebrities who make millions and they have become the role models of America. **Teddy Roosevelt once commented, "The things that will destroy America are prosperity at any price, peace at any price, safety first instead of duty, the love of soft living and the get-rich theory of life."** As we know, in Romans 1-11, Paul outlined the theological foundation for how a person is "justified" by faith in Christ, how one is "satisfied" as he becomes more like Christ. From this point forward, starting in chapter 12, Paul gives us clear instructions of how to live a Christian life.

In this chapter, Paul begins to lay the groundwork for the building of a solid Christian life. Let me ask you a question: Do you want to know how to build a solid Christian life? **Love is the foundation of the Christian life.** Can we be honest? Most of us have learned the art of pretending to love others. We have learned how to smile, speak kindly, and avoid hurting someone's feelings. We even sometimes appear to be moved with compassion over someone else's needs.

Verse 9: *"Love must be sincere."* In other words, **Paul is saying there's no room for phony love.** The love Paul is talking about here is *agape* love. This kind of love only comes from the Lord. Agape love is the love of God. It's the love that God has for us. It's the love that transforms us into the likeness of Christ. If we do not express or show evidence of agape love, we have no claim on eternal life. If agape love does not exist in us, then we are not a true born again believer. 1 John 3:14 tells us, "Anyone who does not love remains in death." 1 Corinthians 13:13 says, "But now abide in faith, hope, and love, but the greatest of these is love."

One day Jesus was about to be put in a trap by a group of religious leaders. First, the Sadducees tried to trap Him, then the Pharisees got together and one of them was an expert in the Law. In Matthew 22:36-40 the Pharisee asked Jesus what the greatest commandment was. Christ's answer was simple: Love God with everything you have and love people. **It's time to stop worrying about all we should do and begin to focus on what we can do to show our love to God and to others.** The Bible is basically summarized in those three verses: Love God, love people and make disciples.

Verse 9b: *"Hate what is evil."* What is the opposite of love? Hate. What is the opposite of holiness? Evil. Proverbs 9:10 says, "To fear the Lord is to hate evil." We must understand the concept of spirit, soul, and body. Our bodies are susceptible to sin. Paul said in Romans 7:14, "I am flesh sold into the bondage of sin. For that which I am doing I do not understand, for I am not practicing what I would like to do, but I am doing the very thing I hate." Remember this: **"Not I, but Christ. I am nothing."** The first step in our walk with the Lord is to recognize that without Christ **we are nothing.** I know I am repeating myself with this concept, but it must sink into who we are and become a part of our lives.

Verse 9c: *"Hold to what is good."* This is not what most of you think. Paul is referring to the spiritual context of life. "Good" is true, pure, honest, and reliable. "Good" does not conform to the world; rather, "good" is what Romans 12:2 means by saying, "Be transformed by the renewing of our minds." God wants us to replace the things of the world with the things of God. There is only one way we can hold onto what is good and that is **to walk in the Spirit of God.** To hold onto the goodness of God means **to be consumed with Jesus.** It means to **remove self** off the throne and **put Christ on the throne.** Most people think of themselves more than they should. That is the very part of us that **must die.** We must turn that part of ourselves over to the Lord to be crucified with Christ. We can't crucify our self. When we die to self, then we can truly understand the unlimited, unconditional love God has for us.

Verse 10a: *"Be devoted to one another in brotherly love."* Do you think you are a loving person? Most of us who think we are loving people are probably more self-centered than we realize. Here's how you can tell: Can you truly love someone who has hurt you, a family member, or one of your children? Can you truly love someone who is your enemy? Can you truly love someone who will never love you back? I've got news for you. No one can display or express this kind of love without the Spirit of God living inside them. This is agape love – a love that can only be implanted in you by the living Christ.

Verse 10b: *"Honor one another above yourself."* Can you give up the most important thing in your life so that someone else can have it? The fact is, the more you have of material things, the harder it is to give them up. At the end of the day, if there's something in your life that you are unwilling to give up if required that something will become an obstacle with your relationship with God. **You see, the Christian life is based on losing, not winning.** You've been taught all your life how much you've got to win. Satan wants you to be a winner in the eyes of the world. Jesus wants you to be a loser of the world so you will gain eternal life. Jesus told the rich young ruler that in order for him to enter into heaven he must sell everything he had and give it to the poor. To gain God's glory, we must come in last place. When Peter asked Him the question, "Which one of us is the greatest?" Jesus told His disciples that it is the one who puts himself last that will come in first place. It's almost guaranteed that whatever awards you win on earth will put you at the back of the line in heaven. I know you've never heard this before because no one wants to deal with the repercussions, but one must understand these concepts before he can really know how Christ operates. It's almost in direct opposition of the world as we know it. We live in a world of false impressions, leading to emptiness.

True love is denying self. True love satisfies our whole heart. God's true love should be at the center of our lives. Without His love, we will fail. The only thing that will ever fill the void in our life is the agape love of God. Our love should originate with God and be channeled to us with His direction. His love is under His will. God's love cannot be found in any entity other than those who have been transformed into His likeness. Many try to receive the true love of God through a person only to find they are let down. **Our whole life should revolve around the love of God.** Does this mean we should not love others? No, not at all! But we should love others for His sake, not ours. Our old self is tied up with "self love." **Self love says, "If you love me, I may love you back, but it will be on my conditions."** Self love says, "My love is based on what you can do for me." When wealthy people go broke, what happens? They lose most of their friends. They come to discover who loves them for who they are as a friend in Christ and not for just their money.

You see, God wants us to crucify all of our old relationships and all we own that is tied to our old self. What does that mean? It means give them over to death and bury all that was evil, not holding onto anything but what is related to God in Christ. Some of us are still holding onto stuff that we need to bury and be resurrected in Christ. When everything is gone, He wants to be the only one left. To truly love God, we must be willing to give up all we have – our money, our time, our families, and ourselves. Self cannot be mixed in with true love. All true love is from God and all true love is God. No longer will we love what our self loves, we will love what God loves. No more will we count our self better than others, but we will see them as our self. At this point we can begin to love others as our self.

CHAPTER 50
TEN OBLIGATIONS FOR OUR CHURCH FAMILY
(Points 1-3)
Romans 12:10-16

"Be devoted to one another in brotherly love. Honor one another above yourselves."- Romans 12:10

The foundation of the Christian faith is love. There are two types of love. The first type of love is controlling or manipulative love, which means it always, wants something in return. This kind of love is conditional love. Conditional love says, "I will love you if…" Conditional love seeks to manipulate with the intent to get what it wants. On the surface it looks real, but it ultimately is covered with self-serving motives. The second type of love is God's love or *agape* love, which is a deep intimate love that says, "I love you and I'm willing to do something on your behalf without receiving any credit or without wanting anything in return." This is unconditional love. This type of love derives out of an intimate relationship with God. It is impossible to develop this type of love on your own.

Christianity is built around two fundamental principles – unconditional love and forgiveness. Most of us think we know what these two principles are, but, the reality is many of us never truly exercise or experience them because we have pretended to love and pretended to forgive for so long. It's hard to pull off the mask and become our real self in Christ. Many of us are walking around with false Christian I.D.'s. Many times it's difficult to know who we really are in Christ. If we are not truly identified in Christ, it is confusing and difficult to discover who we really are. Most of the time we allow our inner selves to be controlled by our personal desires rather than controlled by the will of Christ.

This chapter's lesson starts with verse 10. **Paul outlines for us how God ordained the church for the sole purpose of getting his work done.** As believers, there are fundamental principles we are to apply in our work with other believers in the body of Christ. Paul gives us 10 solid obligations we are to follow as we work together in the unity of Christ. Here are the first three of Paul's "Ten Obligations for Our Church Family".

1) **"Be devoted to one another in brotherly love."** (v. 10a): To be "devoted" means to be "committed to" or "to show allegiance." As Christians, our "devotion" to one another should be a natural form of life. Before one can be "devoted," one must be secure with who one is in Christ. True devotion does not expect anything in return. Love breaks through all barriers. All of man's conflicts are capable of being resolved with love. If both parties will come together in love, conflict can be resolved. John 13:35 says, "By this all men will know that you are my disciples, if you have love for one another." The world is looking at us as we live our lives. The Bible clearly teaches us that our "love" for one another is evident and will be seen. Brotherly love reflects the very nature of Christ Himself. The depth of our brotherly love will determine the depth of our faith in Christ. Love is based on trust. Christian love is based on trust in Christ – trusting in the fact that Christ is really Christ, trusting that Christ is real, and trusting that Christ is alive today. You see, you will never be able to love your brother any deeper than you trust Christ. Without trust, love cannot exist.

2) **"Honor one another above yourselves."** (v. 10b): How do we honor someone above our self? Let's go to Philippians 2:3: "But in humility consider others better than yourselves." Who is our example? Jesus Christ. In Philippians 2:7, Jesus made himself nothing. In verse 8, He humbled Himself. If Jesus made Himself nothing, what should we do? Become nothing, become humble servants. To honor one another, we must do as Jesus

212

did. He obeyed God and served people. This is about our attitude. Some of us may have the attitude that "I'm too good to serve. I don't do commodes. I don't mop floors. I'm too important for that job." Some of us may have the attitude that "I'm embarrassed because that's all I can do. I don't want anyone to see me doing it." Guess what? Both of these attitudes have identified themselves with what they do. What we do does not determine our identity. Let me give you an example. If you are a pastor, think about this concept: In normal conditions you would identify yourself as a pastor, missionary, evangelist, etc. But that's not really who you are. Your real identity is a servant for Christ. All our identities should be established as servants in Christ. Until we can begin to identify ourselves as servants of Christ and have the attitude of Christ, it will be difficult to honor one another above ourselves. We must stop identifying ourselves with our position or job title and consider ourselves as servants of Christ. When we do, everything becomes level at the foot of the cross!

3) **"Never lacking in zeal."** (v. 11): What does this verse mean? How do we have zeal? "Zeal" means to be diligent, to be persistent, and to be self-motivated. Proverbs 18:9 says, "One who is lacking in his work is brother to one who destroys." **There is no substitute for hard work.** Without hard work, very little will be accomplished. But here is the key: How do we work hard for our self and work hard for God, and how do we do it so that we do not become "a workaholic?" Most of us work so much for ourselves we have very little time or energy left over for God. To be zealous in this sense means to be diligent in our work for the Lord. Many times when we do work for the Lord, we do it wanting praise for ourselves. That's not the kind of work Paul is talking about. Because we have been saved by Jesus, and our lives are changed, we have more to be zealous for than a man who does not know Christ.

4) The bottom line is this: To be zealous means to take action. All people have, within themselves, God-given volition. "Volition" is "the act of determining choice or forming a purpose." While God is sovereign, man also has a free will to choose. The zealous will Paul is talking about here is one that is bent against "self" and bent toward "God."

CHAPTER 51

TEN OBLIGATIONS FOR OUR CHURCH FAMILY
(Points 4-6)
Romans 12:10-16

"Be devoted to one another in brotherly love. Honor one another above yourselves."- Romans 12:10

In the last chapter we studied verses 10b and 11a. We discussed the first three points of Paul's 10-point outline regarding the 10 obligations we have to our church family. Let's review the first three.

1) **"Be devoted in brotherly love."** The depth of our brotherly love will be determined by the depth of our love for Christ. Love is based on trust. Without trust, love cannot exist.

2) **"Honor one another above yourselves."** Philippians 2:3 tells us, "But in humility consider others better than yourselves." Christ made Himself nothing, so we must also become nothing so that He can be glorified.

3) **"Never be lacking in zeal."** As Christians, we are to be diligent in the Lord's work. "Zealous" here means "to take action."

In this chapter we will look at the next three points, numbers 4-6:

4) **"Being fervent in spirit."** (v. 11b): The word "fervent" in the Greek is "zeō," which means "almost boiling." The idea here is to be at the point of creating steam, not out of control, but actively pursuing God. Henry Marty, a missionary in India, and my good friend, Wade Akins, both have a fervent spirit. Their hearts' desire is to

"burn out for God." Let's read Galatians 6:9: "Let us not become weary in doing good, for at the proper time we will reap a harvest if we do not give up." If we are not fervent in spirit, we will grow weak and weary.

What does it mean to be fervent in spirit? It means our mind is locked into the things of God. It means that our life principles and our life values are grounded in a love relationship with Christ. We cannot be fervent in spirit if we do not understand that the foundation of the Christian life is love, that God's love for us is unlimited, it is unchangeable, and most of all, it is unconditional. Once we grasp the real concept of love, forgiveness and grace, we are motivated out of an intimate love for God, and not out of duty. Some of us are living for the Lord out of duty. To live out of duty means to live our life by a set of rules and regulations. To live this way is religion. Unsaved people cannot stand religious people, because they see right through them. Religious people are more damaging to the Christian life than hell raisers. You know why? Because they are self-righteous. To be motivated out of love means that we understand God's grace, mercy and forgiveness, and are willing to follow the road map God gave us in His Son, Jesus.

5) **"To serve the Lord."** (v. 11c): Once a person has made a commitment to follow Christ, they then move on to grow as a disciple of Christ. If you are already a disciple of Christ, the next stage is to serve the Lord. Think of it this way: When you join a baseball team, you train, you run, you pitch, you hit, you do drills, you learn signals, and you scrimmage. All for what? To get ready to play the game. God is getting each of us ready for the game. Every time we study God's Word, every time we pray to the Lord, every time we discuss godly things, every time we go through a difficult challenge in our life, God is preparing us for game day. What is game day? The day we are prepared to serve the Lord.

Paul discusses three different kinds of service in chapter 12. First, is the word "latreia," which means "service of worship." Worship is not a one-time event, something we just do on Sundays and Wednesday nights. It's a lifestyle. So, in other words, our lifestyle should always be one of seeking to serve. The second kind of service is "diakonia," which means "practical service." Practical service means to be prepared to serve, not on your terms. Do you know what my problem is? I like to serve, but I like doing it on my terms. But here Paul is trying to teach us to be on red alert to serve. Finally, he uses the Greek word "douleuo," which refers to the service of a bond slave. Paul says, "I am a slave to the Lord, Jesus Christ." To serve the Lord requires us to understand that we are nothing, but Christ is everything. Therefore, we must conclude that within our own power, we cannot accomplish the work He has given us to do. We must seek His help and His strength to serve Him in all things. Paul says in Colossians 1:29, "Striving with His power, which mightily works within me." Your striving need not be for the purpose of achieving. Our striving is for the sole purpose of seeking the power source. Many times we get caught up in the gifts from the Giver and we need to understand our focus should be on the Giver of the gifts.

6) **"Rejoicing in hope."** (v. 12a): What does it mean to rejoice in hope? First, hope is something that cannot be seen. For us to see hope makes hope vanish. To rejoice in hope is humanly impossible. How can we rejoice in hope when we're about to go down financially? How can we rejoice in hope after we've buried someone close to us? How can we rejoice in hope as we're going through a divorce? How do we rejoice in hope when one of our kids is struggling in life? The answer is, we can't. We, within ourselves, cannot rejoice at all. But in Christ, we can always rejoice in hope because of the

promises He has given us. When Christ left us, He left us with all of the tools necessary to make it through life, but that's just the beginning. We can also rejoice in the fact that one day we will serve in our eternal life in heaven.

CHAPTER 52
TEN OBLIGATIONS FOR OUR CHURCH FAMILY
(Points 7-10)
Romans 12:13

"Share with God's people who are in need. Practice hospitality."
- Romans 12:13

In the last chapter we covered points 4, 5, and 6 of the ten obligations Paul outlines to the believers. These obligations are basically Christian precepts that were modeled by our Savior, Jesus Christ. Let's go over the three obligations from last chapter:

4) **"Being fervent in spirit."**

5) **"To serve the Lord."**

6) **"Rejoicing in hope."**

In this chapter we will look at points 7-10. Let's start with point 7.

7) **"Persevering in tribulation"** (v. 12b): If there's anyone who can get through difficult times, it's a Christian. Paul is saying to us that one of the obligations we have as believers is to persevere through the difficulties of life. Let me see if I can break it down for us by asking a question: Why are we required to work through the storms of life? There are several reasons:

   • It develops and matures us into a deeper relationship with Christ.

   • We become dependent on God.

- We are humbled, which forces us to recognize how weak we are.

- When all else fails and there's nothing but God left, then and only then can He get the glory.

Turn to Romans 5:2-5: "Through whom we have gained access by faith into this grace in which we now stand. And we rejoice in the hope of the glory of God. Not only so, but we also rejoice in our sufferings, because we know that suffering produces perseverance; perseverance, character; and character, hope. And hope does not disappoint us, because God has poured out his love into our hearts by the Holy Spirit, whom he has given us." Paul says here that we are to be thankful for our tribulations. Here's why: Trials lead to perseverance, which leads to character, which leads to hope, which will not let us down because God's love is poured out to us through the Holy Spirit. This is important: **The Holy Spirit is the pump that keeps all the spiritual nourishment flowing to you from God.**

Our motto as Christians should be, **"Pain is good."** The crazy thing about it is, no American wants pain. All of us live our lives around staying clear of pain. Why are we so fearful of pain? The more we want to control things, the more fearful we are of losing what we're trying to control. The reason we don't like pain is because we lack a deep trust in the Lord. A person who depends on the Lord and walks by the spirit is a person who does not fear anything in life but God. They are human, they have feelings, but they do not allow their feelings and emotions to control their inner person; rather, their inner person is controlled by the Spirit of the Lord. My hope and prayer is that you and I can grow in the likeness of Christ where we can truly say, "Pain is good," and we mean it. Our culture does not want us to look beyond the concept of "What's in it for me?" God's view of life is much bigger – it expands beyond self and focuses on others.

8) **"Be devoted to prayer."** (v. 12c): One of the main reasons God allows tribulations to happen in our life is so that we can be driven back to God. Prayer is simply talking to God. 1 Thessalonians 5:17 tells us to **"pray without ceasing."** What does that really mean? How can we constantly pray? It's more of an attitude of consistent realization of our true power source. Paul is telling us to be **devoted** to prayer. The word "devoted" means literally "to be strong toward something," "steadfast, unwavering." Adrian Rogers made three points about prayer:

- Prayer should be our first thought, not our last resort.

- Our spiritual life will never rise above our prayer life.

- God always answers prayers that will glorify Himself.

Prayer is the greatest Christian privilege we have. Everything we do should start in prayer. We can do more than pray after we've prayed, but we can't do more than pray until we've prayed. Prayer should be a part of our life just as breathing is a part of our life. In our mind, we are to always be thinking about the things of God. This is constant prayer.

9) **"Contribute to the needs of the saints."** (v. 13a): The last two obligations flow out of living a life for others and not for our self. Let's ask ourselves this question: When was the last time I did something for someone who could not do anything for me in return? In the eyes of the world, we own certain valuable assets, but in God's eyes, we own nothing. We are merely stewards of what He has blessed us with. Jesus made it crystal clear that we have a responsibility to do our best to help anyone in need that we encounter. Galatians 6:10 says,

"Therefore, as we have opportunity, let us do good to all people, especially to those who belong to the family of believers." Paul tells us to do good to all men, but especially those who are of the household of the faith. We have an obligation to take care of our brothers and sisters in Christ. They will see your love through your actions more than through your words.

10) **"Practice hospitality"** (v. 13b): The literal meaning here is to pursue the love of strangers. Hebrews 12:2 tells us, "Do not neglect to show hospitality to strangers." Ok, here it comes: Do you think you practice genuine hospitality? If I were a betting man, I would bet that most people reading this don't really understand what it really means to practice hospitality.

Turn to Luke 14:12-14: "When you give a luncheon or dinner, do not invite your friends or your brothers or your relatives or rich neighbors, lest they will invite you in return and payment come to you. But when you give a reception, invite the poor, the crippled, the lame, and you will be blessed, since they do not have the means to repay you. For you will be repaid at the resurrection of the righteous." Whoever has invited a poor man, a crippled man, a lame man to eat in his home at his table understands what Paul is talking about. Here's the point: Most of us think we are too good to do what Jesus is talking about. We also live in fear. We are afraid that if we invite a poor person over, something in our home may come up missing. If this is the way we're thinking, we're thinking just like a Pharisee and not a Christian. It's time we begin to make the revolutionary change required to change the world. Revolutionary change will not occur without a revolutionary view. Inviting someone to our home or out to eat who cannot repay us will be a revolutionary change for most of us. This change is motivated out of love. Without a deep sense of who we are in Christ, and his unconditional love for us, it will be impossible for us to make such a change. Will you consider allowing Christ to change you into a person who has such a Christ-like revolutionary view of the world?

CHAPTER 53
THE BASIC DUTY OF ALL CHRISTIANS
Romans 12:14-16

"Bless those who persecute you; bless and do not curse."
- Romans 12:14

How many of us think we're doing a good job of living the Christian life? Paul outlines for us a list of basic fundamental principles for all Christians to follow. In this chapter we will explore some very challenging and counter-cultural concepts of the Christian life. These concepts will help us measure our real motives about our Christian walk. If we could outline a few things that we see as important in the Christian faith, what would they be? In verses 14-16, Paul raises the bar and gives us a look at six basic principles of the kind of attitude a real Christian should have in his life.

1) **"Bless those who persecute you."** (v. 14a): Hold on just a minute. Does this verse mean that I must bless someone who hates me? Yes, that is exactly what this verse means. What Paul is really saying here is not only are we to resist hatred and a desire to get even with those who want to harm us, but he is telling us that we are to take an extra step and bless them. What does it mean to bless someone? It means to love them the way Christ loves them. This concept comes straight from Jesus. Turn to Luke 6:27-28: "But I tell you who hear me: Love your enemies, do good to those who hate you, bless those who curse you, pray for those who mistreat you." This is what genuine love looks like in response to being mistreated.

Let's read Luke 6:29-33:

- Give up your coat.

- Give up your shirt.
- Give what is asked of you and don't ask for it back.
- Love those who won't love you back.

This is true Christian love. I hate to say this but most of us think we know what real Christian love is when we really don't. Most of us know what church love, or religious love, is. Church love is, in a way, counterfeit love. It looks good on the outside, but has no depth, no real meaning. God's love is real, authentic, and ever lasting. Church love, or religious love, is a shady kind of love, an "I'm doing this for me" kind of love.

2) **"Bless and do not curse them."** (v. 14b): To reemphasize the point, Paul says don't bless them and then turn around and tell everyone how awful they are. **Anything that's done to make ourselves look good is wrong**. Let me explain what we're talking about. If I were to ask you, in public, if you pray and then ask you if you curse, most of us will agree when asked about prayer. Why? Because we are not afraid to show how religious we are. Our natural tendency is to impress others. When I ask how many of us curse, a few of us would be honest, but most of us would not have the guts to be honest. Why? Because we would not want to be seen as someone who has cursed, which means we want to appear to be religious. The sooner we can appear to be non-religious, the sooner we will become a real, transparent person, one who will not be viewed as self-righteous to non-believers. When we come to Christ we are transformed into His likeness and we receive a new life and a new DNA makeup, which is the DNA of God. At this point we have the capacity to love ourselves and others in His power and His way of love, not ours. However, to do this we must be consumed by Christ.

3) **"Rejoice with those who rejoice."** (v. 15a): This seems simple but most of us fail to exercise this principle. When someone we know celebrates some form of success in the work place, or maybe another child does better than our child, can we truly rejoice with those who rejoice? Most of us have a shade of jealousy. 1 Corinthians 12:26 says, "If one part suffers, every part suffers with it; if one part is honored, every part rejoices with it." In other words, when one person succeeds we should all be joyful. Can we be honest? Some people get excited when something bad happens to someone successful or to someone they want to see fall to their level. Proverbs 17:15 says, "Acquitting the guilty and condemning the innocent - the Lord detests them both." God is displeased when we wish bad things on other people.

4) **"Weep with those who weep."** (v. 15b): James 5:11 says, "As you know, we consider blessed those who have persevered. You have heard of Job's perseverance and have seen what the Lord finally brought about. The Lord is full of compassion and mercy." He is full of compassion. How does this "sense of compassion" look? Let's go to Colossians 3:12: "Therefore, as God's chosen people, holy and dearly loved, clothe yourselves with compassion, kindness, humility, gentleness, and patience." This is what real compassion looks like. If you ever want to answer the question of how a Christian should conduct himself, that's how. God gave us emotions and one of our human emotions is to cry. Never feel like you are a weak person when you cry. To cry is to show your compassion and expose your heart. Being real is part of being a Christian.

5) **"Live in harmony with one another."** (v. 16a): The real Greek meaning here is "to not show impartiality." How many of you think you have this under control?

Let's go to James 2:1-9: "My brother, as believers in our glorious Lord Jesus Christ, don't show favoritism. Suppose a man comes into your meeting wearing a gold ring and fine clothes, and a poor man in shabby clothes also comes in. If you show special attention to the man wearing fine clothes and say, 'Here's a good seat for you,' but say to the poor man, 'You stand there' or 'Sit on the floor by my feet,' have you not discriminated among yourselves and become judges with evil thoughts? Listen, my dear brothers: Has not God chosen those who are poor in the eyes of the world to be rich in faith and to inherit the Kingdom He promised those who love Him? But you have insulted the poor. Is it not the rich who are exploiting you? Are they not the ones who are dragging you into court? Are they not the ones who are slandering the noble name of Him to whom you belong? If you really keep the royal law found in Scripture, 'Love your neighbor as yourself,' you are doing right. But if you show favoritism, you sin and are convicted by the law as lawbreakers."

Ok, what did that verse just say?

- Don't show favoritism.
- Be respectful.
- What you respect you will attract.
- Don't be judgmental.
- Don't display evil thoughts.
- Don't think you are better than anyone else.
- Don't be hypocritical of others.

1 Timothy 5:21 says, "Do nothing in a spirit of partiality." In other words, love those who you find hard to love.

6) **"Do not be proud; be willing to associate with the lowly. Do not be conceited."** (v. 16b): What is the fastest way a person can destroy himself? Pride. Pride is the number one killer in spiritual maturity. It kills, it

destroys, it elevates self, it promotes self, and it loves stroking self. To associate with the lowly means to become humble. Lowly people need help, they need love, and they need support. You may be the only thing that brings a special touch to them. To not be conceited means to humble ourselves to the will of God. Our will is no good. Any man who wants his will to be done over God's will is a conceited person. To be conceited means you think you know everything. Only God knows everything. Will you release self and discover the true meaning of a life in Christ?

CHAPTER 54
HOW TO TREAT YOUR ENEMIES
Romans 12:17-21

"Do not repay anyone evil for evil. Be careful to do what is right in the eyes of everybody. "- Romans 12:17

Have you ever watched the movie "The Secrets of Jonathan Sperry"? It's a movie based on the real life of a man who, I believe, displays for us how to live the way that Paul outlines for us in Romans 12. The movie starts out with four young boys about 12 years old in the 1950's and an older, retired man named Mr. Sperry. Of the four boys, three of them were just your average young men, but the fourth boy was a trouble-maker. During the course of the movie, three of the boys become friends with Mr. Sperry.

One day Mr. Sperry was helping one of the boys work through a difficult problem and he took his Bible and talked to him about the Christian faith. The next week, at the request of Mr. Sperry, the boy brought his friends to Mr. Sperry's home to start a Bible study. Across the street lived a man who was disabled and Mr. Sperry would have one of the boys cut his grass each week. Mr. Sperry told the boy he would pay for cutting his grass but he did not want anyone to know who was paying for it. The old man always asked, "Why are you cutting my grass. I don't need you to do this." The young boy would answer, "I'll do you a good job and have you thought about reading your Bible?"

One day Mr. Sperry died. It crushed the young boy. He was depressed because he had lost a close friend. At that time there was a knock at the door and it was the old man from across the street. He told the boy, "I'm sorry Mr. Sperry died. He was the one paying to cut my lawn, wasn't he?" The boy said, "Yes." The old man said, "Well, I still want you to cut my grass under one condition. You let me pay you for cutting my yard." Then he said,

"Mr. Sperry was a good Christian man," and he closed by saying, "and I've been reading my Bible," and walked out the door. The mother of the boy was in the room and tears streamed from her eyes. The young boy said, "Mom, why are you crying?" She said, "This is incredible that the old man would come over and share about Mr. Sperry." He asked, "Why?" She said, "Because many years ago the old man had a car accident and his car hit and killed Mr. Sperry's wife." This is supernatural living. How do you love someone who has killed someone in your family? Mr. Sperry showed God's love in a practical, but supernatural way – not under his power, but under the Lordship of Christ. This chapter deals with this very issue. Paul's view of how to live the Christian life grows to include loving our enemies.

1) **"Do not repay anyone evil for evil."** (v. 17a): Stop getting mad and getting even. Paul says we are never to pay back evil for evil. 1 Peter 3:8-9 says, "Finally, all of you, live in harmony with one another; be sympathetic, love as brothers, be compassionate and humble. Do not repay evil with evil or insult with insult, but with blessing, because to this you were called so that you may inherit a blessing." This tells us to go the extra mile. As Christians, we are to repay with blessings. Here's the concept: As you bless others, God will bless you. Could this be the log jam of your Christian life?

2) **"Be careful to do what is right in the eyes of everybody."** (v. 17b): What you respect, you will attract. Paul tells us to respect what is right. The word "right" in the Greek is "kalos," which means instinctively good, proper, and honest. He wants us to visibly be doing the right thing. If we live a life of forgiveness with others, we are allowing Christ to express Himself in and through our lives.

3) **"If it is possible, as far as it depends on you, live at peace with everyone."** (v. 18): To be at peace requires both sides to want peace. Paul says, "As far as it depends on you." In other words, we can't control anyone else but ourselves, but we need to make sure we are striving for peace. **Before we can be at peace with others, we must be at peace with our self and with God.** Peace and love are harmonious. You must also learn to love yourself before you can love someone else. Be careful not to draw lines in the sand and say, "I can't stand this person because he disagrees with me about religion, politics, etc." You can be at peace with someone and also disagree with them.

4) **"Do not take revenge, my friends, but leave room for God's wrath, for it is written: 'It is mine to avenge; I will repay,' says the Lord."** (v. 19): Never try to be the enforcer. That's God's job. Paul is telling us that, regardless of how serious or harmful the offense, we never have the right to render punishment ourselves. This is difficult to live out, because our natural response is, "I will take the law into my own hands;" but it is also sound Biblical truth. God can be trusted to dole out judgment in his time.

5) **"On the contrary: 'If your enemy is hungry, feed him; if he is thirsty, give him something to drink. In doing this, you will heap burning coals on his head.' Do not be overcome by evil, but overcome evil with good."** (vv. 20-21): Give of yourself and overcome evil. Paul is quoting from Proverbs 25:21-22: "If your enemy is hungry, give him food to eat; if he is thirsty, give him water to drink. In doing this, you will heap burning coals on his head, and the LORD will reward you." The phrase "a burning heap of coals upon his

233

head" refers to an old Egyptian custom of making a public declaration of contrition by carrying a pan of burning coals on one's head to repent the burning pain of shame and guilt. The key to overcoming evil is twofold: Go out of your way to be kind to your enemies, and when you show God's love to someone who is your enemy, you will shame them from their hatred with your love. Why? Because you allow Christ to be expressed through your life.

CHAPTER 55
SUBMISSION TO THE AUTHORITIES
Romans 13:1-3

"Everyone must submit himself to the governing authorities, for there is no authority except that which God has established. The authorities that exist have been established by God."
- Romans 13:1

Have you ever gotten to the point that you ignore the government and even blame the government for the problems in your life? Every day the news media brings us mostly bad news about our government and often times we get entrenched in it only to develop an attitude of bitterness toward our political leaders. In this chapter we move into the clearest, most specific New Testament teaching on the Christian's responsibility to civil authority. As we know, starting with Romans chapter 12, Paul reveals to us how to live a Christian life. The first verse deals with **our relationship with God**. Verses 3-16 deal with **our relationships with other Christians**. Verses 17-21 deal with **our relationships with unbelievers and our enemies.** This chapter deals with **our relationship with governing authorities**. What do you believe our role is as Christians in government? How many of you believe you have a pretty good balance in your life when it comes to politics? Do you think about the government and politics more than you do about the gospel?

More than likely, if you answer that question honestly, it will show you that your life is actually out of balance. Why? Because the reality is we are more concerned about the government and consumed with politics than we are with God. As we review the next verse of Scripture, I want us to observe this issue from a different perspective. The goal of the church is not to change our society, but to worship, serve, and multiply the things above this world and not become consumed with the world. Does that mean that I must live separated from the world? No. The critical question becomes, "What consumes my life?" Anything other than God, including politics, causes us to have a wrong perspective of the world.

Paul says in verse 1, *"Everyone must submit himself to the governing authorities, for there is no authority except that which God has established. The authorities that exist have been established by God."* Paul is giving us a command here. Turn to Matthew 22:21: "Then he said to them, 'Give to Caesar what is Caesar's, and to God what is God's.'" What does it mean to give Caesar the things that are Caesar's? **Effective godly living has an impact on others around you.** What is our #1 priority as Christians? Turn to Mark 16:15:"He said to them, 'Go into all the world and preach the good news to all creation.'"

If we thought about Christ as much as we talk about politics, what would happen? Politics ultimately is an opinion. The gospel is ultimately man's salvation through Christ's sacrifice. However, we must follow the order provided by God. Turn to 1 Peter 2:11-13: "Dear friends, I urge you, as aliens and strangers in the world, to abstain from sinful desires, which war against your soul. Live such good lives among the pagans that, though they accuse you of doing wrong, they may see your good deeds and glorify God on the day he visits us. Submit yourselves for the Lord's sake to every authority instituted among men: whether to the king, as the supreme authority." Paul uses very strong language here to make his point. He says, "Dear friends, I urge you." In other words, he is saying, **I have a duty to love those who love me first and I should reciprocate God's love by living for Him**.

He then says to his audience, "as aliens and strangers." The Greek word for "aliens" is translated "alongside the house." It denotes any person who lives in a country not his own and, therefore, is a foreigner. The term fits Christians who do not belong to this world's system, but live alongside those who do. Philippians 3:20 says, "For our citizenship is in heaven, from which also we eagerly wait for a Savior, the Lord Jesus Christ." The reality is that our real documents need to be stamped "heaven." We can have it all worked out in the world's eyes, but heaven is our home.

Paul then tells us to abstain from fleshly lusts. Since we are not part of this world, we have been given the tools required to abstain because of the indwelling of the Holy Spirit. "Which wage war against the soul" (v. 11). This conveys the fact that we will struggle within ourselves. To "wage war" is a military term meaning "to carry out a military campaign." Paul is really saying we have a civil war going on inside of us. Our flesh or body is always in conflict with our spirit. Why? God's Spirit is pure and our body is connected to our "old self." If the old self has not been put to death completely, it will come into opposition with the spirit. Go to verse 13: "Submit yourselves" means to arrange in formation with the commander. God expects us to submit ourselves to the human institutions God ordained. Why do we follow? "For the Lord's sake." Paul tells us that motivation for us submitting to authority is for the Lord's sake. As Christians, we obey earthly authority to honor God's authority. Will you honor your government because of the Lord? At the end, is God in control of the things in your world that seem out of control? The answer is yes. If this is true, we can rest in peace that we must give Him our love and trust and learn to fully depend on Him in all things.

CHAPTER 56
LOVE: THE KEY TO THE CHRISTIAN LIFE
Romans 13:8-10

"Let no debt remain outstanding, except the continuing debt to love one another, for he who loves his fellow man has fulfilled the law."- Romans 13:8

If I were to ask you what is the most important aspect of the Christian life, what would be your response? Paul addresses this very subject matter in this chapter. Let's look at verse 8, *"Let no debt remain outstanding, except the continuing debt to love one another, for he who loves his fellow man has fulfilled the law."*

As we discussed in earlier chapters on several occasions, the key to the Christian life is **love**. What is the fundamental purpose of the Christian life? Turn to John 4:34: "'My food,' said Jesus, 'is to do the will of Him who sent me and to finish his work.'" If the purpose of Christ was to do the will of the Father, what is our purpose? Turn to John 6:38: "For I have come down from heaven not to do my will but to do the will of him who sent me." **The key to the Christian life is love. The purpose of the Christian life is to do the will of God.**

To follow the will of God we must obey the Holy Spirit and exercise faith in our walk with the Lord. What causes man to disobey? Ephesians 4:22 tells us, "You were taught, with regard to your former way of life, to put off your old self, which is being corrupted by its deceitful desires." **Disobedience usually manifests itself in self**. A renewed life in Christ has a disposition that is inspired by the Holy Spirit to follow the will of God. Paul said in Romans 7:22, "For in my inner being I delight in God's law." Paul is leading us to my main point, which is that love is the key to all godly obedience. Why? Because love fulfills the law.

Paul says in verse 8, *"Owe nothing to anyone except in Christian love."* Proverbs 19:17 says, "He who is kind to the poor lends to the LORD, and he will reward him for what he has done." This tells us that, "Whomever is gracious to the poor lends to the Lord." Now, you mean to tell me that whatever I do for the poor is like doing it for the Lord? Let's go to Matthew 5:42: "Give to the one who asks you, and do not turn away from the one who wants to borrow from you." To owe nothing except in love means that the debt of love is continuous. We will always have the debt of love hanging over our heads. In other words we will never be able to pay off the debt of love we owe to the people we come in contact with.

We are to show the love of Christ everywhere we go. How many of you want more love? What we plant is what we get back in a crop. If we never love we will never receive love. John 13:34-35 says, "'A new command I give you: Love one another. As I have loved you, so you must love one another. By this all men will know that you are my disciples, if you love one another.'" Our focus is directed to the love of Christ. If we ask ourselves to what level do we love, the answer would be to the same extent Christ extended his love to others. 1 John 4:7 says, "Dear friends, let us love one another, for love comes from God. Everyone who loves has been born of God and knows God."

When you came to Christ, your love switch was turned on. Your ability to love someone who cannot love you back is a love that can only come from God.

Agape love is the unconditional love that comes from God. The cool thing about God's love is that He will never force His love on us. His love is unchangeable. There's nothing that we can do that will keep Him from loving us. His love is unlimited. We cannot imagine the depth and height of God's love. 1 Peter 1:22 says, "Now that you have purified yourselves by obeying the truth so that you have sincere love for your brothers, love one another deeply, from the heart." Godly love is more than an emotion or feeling. It begins with compassion, kindness, humility, gentleness, and patience. Godly love is to speak truth, but always with grace and humility. Godly love is never self-serving. Godly love never causes another brother to stumble. Godly love is forgiving.

Ephesians 4:32 tells us, "Be kind and compassionate to one another, forgiving each other, just as in Christ God forgave you." Godly love is gentleness, it's humility, it's patience, it's not jealous, it's not arrogant, it's not selfish. Godly love never fails. 1 Corinthians 13:4-8, "Love is patient, love is kind. It does not envy, it does not boast, it is not proud. It is not rude, it is not self-seeking, it is not easily angered, and it keeps no record of wrongs. Love does not delight in evil but rejoices with the truth. It always protects, always trusts, always hopes, and always perseveres. Love never fails. But where there are prophecies, they will cease; where there are tongues, they will be stilled; where there is knowledge, it will pass away." How do we know if we have godly love? When we are willing to sacrifice our own needs for the needs of someone else who can never repay us.

Can I be honest? Most all of us have godly love in us, however, we fail to intentionally initiate His love through God's Spirit. We have all the tools. God supplies us with all we need when we come to Him in faith and become a Christian. We have the resources but we strive to change ourselves only to find that we fail. Okay, let's look at it this way. Where does love originate? From God in Christ. How does His love come to us? By grace. We don't earn it. We don't deserve it. God graces us with a well of love. The well is deep and will never run dry. How many of you have ever gotten water out of a well?

I remember when I was young, at my grandparents' house in the 1960's, priming the pump and getting water by pushing up and down to pump water. God's well is unlimited with His love. Now watch this. How does His love get to us? Through the Holy Spirit. The Holy Spirit is the pump that supplies God's love to us. Romans 5:5 says, "And hope does not disappoint us, because God has poured out his love into our hearts by the Holy Spirit, whom he has given us." God has a well full of His love for us that we receive through the Holy Spirit.

When we do we will surrender all hatred, bitterness, pride, and revenge to the lordship of Christ and we will be supplied with the agape love of God. In closing, godly love is a choice. Paul says in Colossians 3:14, "And over all these virtues put on love, which binds them all together in perfect unity." Godly love is rejuvenating. Will you join me today in allowing God to restore you with the power of His love?

CHAPTER 57
PUT ON THE CLOTHES OF CHRIST
Romans 13:11-14

"Rather, clothe yourselves with the Lord Jesus Christ, and do not think about how to gratify the desires of the sinful nature."
- Romans 13:14

In the last chapter we discovered that love is the foundation of the Christian faith. Love is an action. Love is not a feeling. We often confuse love with emotion; however, God's love is more powerful than human emotions. Why? Because He loved us while we were messed up sinners. He had no reason to love us. He does not even need us but, because of His love, He cares and wants us to be set free from all of our nasty baggage.

In the late 70's I played high school football. My linebacker coach would always tell us to "stay on ready to keep from getting ready." The message in this chapter deals with the second coming of Christ and how we are to be prepared as Christians. We need to "stay on ready" for God to keep from having to get ready. The word "Christian" is a very unpopular word in today's world. 1 Peter 4:16 says, "However, if you suffer as a Christian, do not be ashamed, but praise God that you bear that name." He is basically saying, if we are made fun of because of our faith in Christ, we should consider it a badge of honor. We are not to be ashamed because it identifies us with the Lord Jesus Christ and, therefore, brings honor and glory to Christ in our suffering.

Verse 11: *"And do this, understanding the present time. The hour has come for you to wake up from your slumber, because our salvation is nearer now than when we first believed."* Paul is saying, "Wake up." In other words, as Christians, we are to be "on call" 24/7. Now what does "on call" mean? It means to be waiting with anticipation, ready to serve. Paul is saying here we need to wake up because we are "on call." If we're not awake, what are we? Asleep. Now what kind of sleep were the Christians in at this time? They were spiritually asleep. Often times I spiritually go to sleep because I focus on myself and become consumed by some other external crisis.

Ephesians 5:15 tells us; "For it is light that makes everything visible. This is why it is said: 'Wake up, O sleeper, rise from the dead, and Christ will shine on you.'" Who was Paul talking to in this verse? The saved or the unsaved? The saved. He was talking to those who were Christians but spiritually dead. Can we be blind but alive? Can we be a Christian but be spiritually blind? When we have a group of family members coming to our house, what do we do? Cut the grass, clean the house, vacuum the floor, dust the furniture, and clean out the refrigerator. Why? Because we want to get ready for our guests. Some people wait and put off ever cleaning their home. Others always keep it clean and they are always ready to have a guest. My mother is always ready. She is anticipating guests at any time. My grandmother was the same way. If you were passing through town, she wanted you to stop so she could feed you. She stayed "on call." She stayed "on ready" to keep from getting ready.

Verses 12-13: *"The night is nearly over; the day is almost here. So let us put aside the deeds of darkness and put on the armor of light. Let us behave decently, as in the daytime, not in orgies and drunkenness, not in sexual immorality and debauchery, not in dissension and jealousy."* The night is sin. The day is Christ. We do not know when the return of Christ will be, but the point is that, like my grandmother, we should always be ready to see the Lord. Paul says put aside darkness. In other words, stop sinning. If we have Christ in our life, we have all we need to stop sinning. It is important to realize that you have the power of Christ in you to stop sinning.

Ephesians 4:30 says, "And do not grieve the Holy Spirit of God, with whom you were sealed for the day of redemption." This verse emphasizes that the Lord is grieved by our sin. Sin is a choice. Paul goes on to tell us to "Lay aside sin." In this way, we

244

are to take off the clothes of sin. Ephesians 4:22 says, "You were taught, with regard to your former way of life, to put off your old self, which is being corrupted by its deceitful desires." This verse says, "Lay aside the old self." Colossians 3:8-9, "But now you must rid yourselves of all such things as these: anger, rage, malice, slander, and filthy language from your lips. Do not lie to each other, since you have taken off your old self with its practices." This one says, "Lay aside the old self with its evil practices." Always remember, "old self" equals evilness. Hebrews 12:1 says, "Therefore, since we are surrounded by such a great cloud of witnesses, let us throw off everything that hinders and the sin that so easily entangles, and let us run with perseverance the race marked out for us." This verse tells us to "Lay aside our sin." Ephesians 6:11 says, to "put on the armor of God," meaning to prepare for war. We are in a spiritual battle. Without the armor of God, we will not be able to withstand the darts of Satan. Through the Holy Spirit, we have a power source that will give us the resources to overcome our burdens. What does it mean "to behave decently?" To live in a way that pleases God. 2 Peter 3:14, "So then, dear friends, since you are looking forward to this, make every effort to be found spotless, blameless and at peace with him." As Christians we are to live outside the ways of the world. Paul outlines several special sins:

1) Orgies
2) Drunkenness
3) Sexual immorality
4) Sexual promiscuity
5) Dissension (meaning bickering, petty disagreements, to overcome and conquer at the expense of others)
6) Jealousy (meaning envy)

Verse 14: *"Rather, clothe yourselves with the Lord Jesus Christ, and do not think about how to gratify the desires of the sinful nature."* Paul tells us to put on Christ. Philippians 3:13-14 says, "Brothers, I do not consider myself yet to have taken hold of it. But one thing I do: Forgetting what is behind and straining toward what is ahead, I press on toward the goal to win the prize for which God has called me heavenward in Christ Jesus." This tells us to "pursue the goal of Christ-likeness." So, how do we put on Christ?

When I was six years old, I loved Superman. Every Saturday morning I would lay in the floor, arranging myself as close to the 19" black and white TV as possible to watch Superman. I dreamed of one day having the powers of Superman, but I knew I could not have his powers until I had the Superman cape uniform. On my sixth birthday, my mother made me my first and only official Superman cape. It was bright blue with the red "S" sown in the center of the cape. Following the birthday celebration and just after eating birthday cake, I put on my Superman cape. I had this unbelievable sense of confidence. I truly believed I had supernatural powers. I knew I would need to get used to my new abilities so I decided to start with something simple, I decided to fly around the living room. I perched myself on the top of the couch, bracing myself with the wall behind me. I jumped and attempted to fly around the room. I truly believed my power was in the cape. When I jumped, I flew for just about half a second, then gravity took over and my head hit the corner of the coffee table. The next thing I knew, I was at the doctor's office, getting stitches in my sock feet while missing two front teeth. I was a sight to behold. Obviously, the power was not in the cape.

Many of us think our power is in our self and in our abilities, but we always fail because we do not realize our true power source. Many of us try to fly on the efforts of self. Our power source, as Christians, is Jesus Christ. To put on Christ means to allow the Holy Spirit to transform us into His likeness, in other words we become like Christ. We are to clothe ourselves in Christ. We are to integrate our lives with Christ. To conclude, we are not to gratify the needs of our sinful nature. How do we do that? Galatians 5:16 has the answer: "So I say, live by the Spirit, and you will not gratify the desires of the sinful nature." The only way we can stay out of sin is to "live by the Spirit." Living by the Spirit is talking to God, thinking about God, talking to others about God, trusting God for the provisions of life, trusting God for His promises, praying to God, serving God, loving God, loving people, and making disciples. Will you make a commitment today to stay on ready to keep from getting ready? Will you allow yourself to be consumed by the things of God and be lead by the Spirit of God?

CHAPTER 58
THE WEAK AND THE STRONG
Romans 14:1-4

"Accept him whose faith is weak, without passing judgment on disputable matters."- Romans 14:1

Do you believe that the power of sin is real? The Bible teaches us clearly that every Christian should assess where they are in their walk with the Lord. Each of us should make an evaluation of where we are in our spiritual journey. If you woke up this morning and you have blood running through your veins, God has a plan for your life. Turn to 1 Corinthians 11:28: "A man ought to examine himself before he eats of the bread and drinks of the cup." Paul is telling the Christians to examine themselves. Why is an examination of oneself an important part of our spiritual development? When we take inventory of our life and compare who we really are to who Christ is, we realize our faults and humbly admit our shortcomings.

The hardest thing for men to do is to admit we're wrong. The easiest thing for us to do is to criticize someone else's mistakes, their faults and frailties; but to subject our self to the admission of wrongness is to be totally submissive to another person. It is this kind of forgiveness that God is looking for from us. Turn to 2 Corinthians 7: "Since we have these promises, dear friends, let us purify ourselves from everything that contaminates body and spirit, perfecting holiness out of reverence for God." Paul points out to us that we are to "cleanse ourselves from the defilements of the flesh." **The first step in the process is to recognize our weakness.**

The second step is to come clean with God. The third step is to ask for forgiveness. Let's read Romans 14:1-4: *"Accept him whose faith is weak, without passing judgment on disputable matters. One man's faith allows him to eat everything, but another man, whose faith is weak, eats only vegetables. The man who eats everything must not look down on him who does not, and the man who does not eat everything must not condemn the man who does, for God has accepted him. Who are you to judge someone else's servant? To his own master he stands or falls. And he will stand, for the Lord is able to make him stand.* " Do you know any weak Christians? What is Paul saying here? None of us are better than anyone else. So, if none of us are better than the other, where does that put you with your friend who is struggling with alcohol, drugs, or porn? If you struggle in these areas, understand that you are weak. Why are you weak? **You're weak because you've allowed the passionate desires of self to overthrow the Spirit of the Lord.** At times, we are all weak, but, as Christians, we have the tools inside of us required to overcome the sin in our life. What we cannot understand, we can endure with God. The point here is this – regardless of where you are in your life, work with and love all people in the attitude of Christ. Every person needs another person to mentor them in the ways of the Christian walk. Paul outlines for us four reasons why we should receive all believers, regardless of where they are in their faith:

1) **Because God receives us**. God first loved us. He received us when we were not worth receiving and, because God did that for us, we must follow the same behavior. Sometimes it's tough receiving someone who dislikes us. We are not to judge others by what's happening in their lives. If we do, we become heartless and lose sense of reality. Too often we make judgments about people based on their looks or their behavior. Most people who have behavior issues have something internal that they have never given over to the Lord. Acts 10:28, "He said to them: 'You are well aware that it is against our law for a Jew to associate with a Gentile or visit him. But God has shown me that I should not call any man impure or unclean.'" Peter makes it clear that, regardless of who we are, God wants us to associate with everyone. Romans 8:38-39 says, "For I am convinced that neither death nor life, neither angels nor demons, neither the present nor the

future, nor any powers, neither height nor depth, nor anything else in all creation, will be able to separate us from the love of God that is in Christ Jesus our Lord." You may be the closest thing to God for the person who is struggling with certain issues. When I get to heaven and my life is laid out before me, I can only imagine all the many times I failed to minister to those God had arranged to be put right in front of me. Sadly, in those moments, I missed an opportunity to do the will of God, which resulted in me missing a blessing, all because I was too focused on myself.

2) **Because God gives all of us strength.** Our strength comes from God. All good things come from the Lord. 1 Peter 1:5, "Who through faith are shielded by God's power until the coming of the salvation that is ready to be revealed in the last time." The Bible tells us that we are protected by the power of God. God is our power source. Every ounce of strength comes from Him. We are nothing without Him.

3) **Because God is sovereign and fulfills His promises.** We help others because God promises us heavenly rewards for helping others. Colossians 2:16-17 says, "Therefore do not let anyone judge you by what you eat or drink, or with regard to a religious festival, a New Moon celebration or a Sabbath day. These are a shadow of the things that are to come; the reality, however, is found in Christ." Everything about our lives is integrated in Christ. If not, we will be separated from the Lord.

4) **Because God will judge all believers.** Every person will have to give an account to God for all he has done. Philippians 2:10-11 says, "That at the name of Jesus every knee should bow, in heaven and on earth and under the earth, and every tongue confess that Jesus Christ is Lord, to the glory of God the Father." Every knee shall bow and every tongue shall confess that Jesus Christ is Lord. And on that day, guess what? We will not be held accountable for anyone else, but we will be held accountable for ourselves. Regardless of who you are, you will bow down to the living Christ and you will confess to the lordship of Christ. Here's the issue: Have you told your friends and family about Christ? There will come a time when it's too late for those in need.

CHAPTER 59
THE LORDSHIP OF CHRIST
Romans 14:9-12 (2 Cor. 5:5-15)

"For this very reason, Christ died and returned to life so that he might be the Lord of both the dead and the living."- Romans 14:9

What does it mean to be the lord of something? What is lordship? To understand what lordship is, we need to know what the word means. Since I know the word "lord" was an Old English word, I looked up the word "lordship" in my 1828 American dictionary of the English language, written by Mr. Webster. "Lord" means "a master, a person possessing supreme power and authority." In the Old Testament, the word "Lord" is translated as "Jehovah, the Supreme Being." In 1 Corinthians, Christ is called the "Lord of glory." In Revelation, Christ is called the "Lord of Lords." So what is lordship? Lordship is living in the authority of the supreme power and grace of Jesus Christ.

Turn to 2 Corinthians 5:5-15. If we are Christians, this life is temporary. Our real life lies ahead of us. Verse 5: For what purpose did God make us? *"Now it is God who has made us for this very purpose and has given us the Spirit as a deposit, guaranteeing what is to come."* God's Spirit is a down payment or security deposit for guaranteeing us the payoff of heaven. Not only is our Lord powerful, but he also cares. He gave us the Holy Spirit as a down payment while we are here on earth.

Verse 6: *"Therefore we are always confident and know that as long as we are at home in the body we are away from the Lord."* There are three parts to a person. What are they? Body, soul and spirit. "We are at home in the body," means to be hooked up with your flesh and consumed with yourself, therefore, you are disconnected from God.

Verse 7: *"We live by faith, not by sight."* Let's talk about what that means. If we see it then it's not faith. Faith is built on hope and confidence that God is who He says He is and can do what He says He can do. Faith is built on hope and confidence in Christ as the supreme power and authority in one's life. **Lordship** is when we understand His authority and we live with the intensity of who he really is as ruler of the world. **Lordship** is when we give up total control of ourselves and seek for Him to take control over our lives. **Lordship** is when we replace our inner will with the will of the Lord.

Verse 8: *"We are confident, I say, and would prefer to be away from the body and at home with the Lord."* What do you want to be? Do you want to live a life in the world or a life following and trusting God? Many talk about Christ. They identify going to church as service. Going to church has nothing to do with service. Most of us Christians don't have a clue what it means to live a life in Christ. Some of us have done ministry and some of us are preachers, teachers, and deacons, but never have lived a life where Christ is the Lord of our life. Some of us think service is living for Christ. We may sing in the choir, teach, or do evangelism, and we even feel good about our service. We see Christ more as a safety net, so when things go wrong we can pray to Christ. In a way He is our Savior, but in many ways we have not declared him Lord. It's like we've gone through the process of becoming a Christian, but we don't think we can handle living every day for Christ. Sometimes we treat our relationship with the Lord like buying an extra medical emergency bag. We will have it if we ever really need it, but as long as nothing happens then we're okay.

Here's what I believe – and it's a shocker: There are just as many **unsaved** people who act like Jesus as saved people who act like Jesus. Let me explain. When is the last time you invited a person of another race into your home? Jesus did. When is the last time you helped a person with an addiction? Jesus did. When is the last time you gave a helping hand to a homeless person? Jesus did. You see, I know a lot of people who talk the message of Christ and write the books about what they've seen and done, but I only know of a few who have truly lived for Christ. To live for Christ means to feel the pain of the person, to try to understand his condition, and to truly help him in all aspects of life. Christ took a holistic, but simplified approach to solving all the complicated issues of a man.

Most Christians want to be backseat preachers or judge junkies. We can tell people what they should do, but Christ wants us to live and be like Him. To live means to show. To live means to help. To live means to laugh. To live means to cry. To live means to hurt while sacrificing for others. To live means to rejoice, even when things go wrong. To live means to give a man a drink when he's thirsty. To live means to feed a man when he's hungry. To live means to help someone other than ourselves. To live in Christ is to die to our self. **The Gospel is expressed more by how we live than by how we tell others to live.**

Verse 9: *"So we make it our goal to please him, whether we are at home in the body or away from it."* The number one goal of every person's life should be to please God. So why do we always want to please people? God's not interested in what we want. He's only interested in what He wants us to do for Him. Pleasing God requires us to transform how we think. Most of us think of ourselves too highly. Some of us seem to think we know everything. God wants us to see things the way Christ sees them.

Verse 10: *"For we must all appear before the judgment seat of Christ, that each one may receive what is due him for the things done while in the body, whether good or bad."* Circle the word "all" here. Every person will be held accountable for what they have done. Some may say that they have done nothing wrong. Some may say they have been an awful person. The reality is, it doesn't matter what you think or anyone else thinks. It only matters what God thinks. Most of us tie our self worth to our net worth. If you were to lose 50% of your net worth, how would it make you feel? Would you be depressed? I am guilty of doing this. What God has shown me is that what I have does not determine who I am, or my identity. The right answer is: **Christ + I am Nothing = Christian.** Regardless of where we are in life, God is calling each of us into a deeper relationship with Him. Many church people get confused. They seek more religion. If I can say all the right things, I will camouflage who I really am. I appear to be religious, but I'm really a pretender. A pretender is really a phony. A phony is a pretend Christian with a fake ID. We don't need more religion. We need a deeper relationship with Christ. Every man will stand before God and be judged on what he has done.

Verse 11: *"Since, then, we know what it is to fear the Lord, we try to persuade men. What we are is plain to God, and I hope it is also plain to your conscience."* To fear the Lord is to know His power. How many of you fear the Lord? The word "fear" really means "to revere or respect and trust the Lord." If I were a betting man, I would bet most of us don't fear the Lord. Why? Because if we truly respected the Lord, we would not go to strip clubs, watch porn, do drugs, drink like a fish, waste money gambling, cheat on our taxes, be selfish, and talk about each other.

Verse 15: *"And he died for all, that those who live should no longer live for themselves but for him who died for them and was raised again."* Christ died for all. What was Paul saying? No man is greater than another man. No man has more value over another man. What does it mean when he says, "Those who should no longer live for themselves"? Paul was informing his reader that when Christ died on the cross, the whole deal changed. There was no reason to live for yourself. Here's the crazy part of this equation: Christ has died for us. We have heard the message, but we continue to live for ourselves. Who wants to live a life of bitterness, hatred, and unhappiness? If you do, it's easy. Live your life for yourself, think of yourself first, feel sorry for yourself, and focus on your problems and you will be consumed with yourself.

The hardest thing for us to do when everything seems to be going wrong is to not focus on our problems. When we focus on Christ, we are set free from everything else. We will never escape suffering. It's a process of life. Suffering either kills us or it grows us. Following Christ does not stop the suffering. It just reminds us how weak we are and how powerful God is. It is also comforting to know that He is walking with us through whatever issue we have. His Word gives us the promise of eternal life. There is no promise of a comfortable life when following Christ. A comfortable life is a false concept created mostly by performance-based Americans who see God as a crisis manager. Will you consider making Christ the Lord of your life?

CHAPTER 60
PLEASE GOD, NOT PEOPLE
Romans 15:1-6

"We who are strong ought to bear with the failings of the weak and not to please ourselves."- Romans 15:1

The unity of God's people creates a spiritual oneness that ultimately affects the lives of all believers. This chapter will help us look at how we should draw from each other to strengthen our faith in the Lord. God's overall plan is for us to transform outwardly into what he want us to be inwardly. It's like the transformation process of popcorn. Popcorn starts with just a kernel of corn, which is then heated up to a high temperature. When the temperature of the corn heats the moisture inside the kernel, it expands the inside core of the corn, causing it to burst out of its shell. In other words, what is on the inside exposes itself on the outside. Every Christian is like popcorn.

There is an order to God's plan. The first step of His plan requires us to understand that we must relinquish all of our rights and become submissive to the authority of Christ. The second step of His plan is for us to find strength in the Lord through each other. How does this occur? When we are saved, we receive the gift of the Holy Spirit that creates a spiritual unity among those who believe in Christ. The Power of God's Holy Spirit is essential for us to strengthen one another.

Let's read Acts 4:34-35: "There were no needy persons among them. For from time to time those who owned lands or houses sold them, brought the money from the sales and put it at the apostles' feet, and it was distributed to anyone as he had need." How do we solve meeting the needs of others? By the government? By volunteer organizations? These do serve people, but at the end of the day, it's the people in the church.

Peter 3:8 says, "Finally, all of you, live in harmony with one another; be sympathetic, love as brothers, be compassionate and humble." In the Christian life, there's no room for critical views, racial statements, and talking down to others. As Christians, we must show brotherly love, kindness, and humbleness in spirit. To do this, we must be intoxicated. To do this we must come under the influence. You are thinking now, "This guy has lost his mind." Turn to 1 Corinthians 12:13: "For we were all baptized by one Spirit into one body—whether Jews or Greeks, slave or free—and we were all given the one Spirit to drink." Paul says, "And we were all made to drink of one Spirit!" Paul is telling us here to become intoxicated and under the influence of the Holy Spirit.

You see, if a person is intoxicated with alcohol, they become another person. You take a sober, shy guy like Clark Kent. He doesn't talk much. Get him intoxicated and he transforms into a Mr. Know-It-All. He thinks he's Superman. I remember back in my college days, when I would get intoxicated, I felt bigger than life. It allowed me to become the person I always wanted to be. Why? Because my inhibitions were gone. Paul is telling us as Christians there's no need to be under a temporary influence. If we are empowered by the Holy Spirit and become intoxicated with the power of God, we will transform into the real person God has always wanted us to become. God actually designed us to function in this way.

Turn to 1 John 1:7: "But if we walk in the light, as he is in the light, we have fellowship with one another, and the blood of Jesus, his Son, purifies us from all sin." What does it mean to walk in the light? How do we walk in the light? **To walk in the light requires us to live in the light.** To live in the light means for us to be connected to the power source at all times. Our power source is Christ. He is our authority. He is our Savior. He is our Lord. He is our Master. He is our Creator. He is our hope. He is our peace. He is our joy. He is our truth. He is our light. He is our everything. He is our friend. His name is Jesus, the Christ. Jesus is off the hook. He is bad to the bone. He is real, He is alive, and He wants to live in your heart and take control of your life. Will you allow Him to be all of the above in your life today? If so, simply get on your knees and ask the Lord to take total control of your life. Confess to Him all the baggage in your life. Let Him know how weak you are without Him. Ask Him to show you His ways and to give you strength, courage, and peace. When you are on your knees you don't have far to fall.

CHAPTER 61
ACCEPTING OTHERS
Romans 15:7-13

"Accept one another, then, just as Christ accepted you, in order to bring praise to God."- Romans 15:7

The way we view the world determines how we view people, and the way we view people is how we view the world. Each of us comes to the dance with our own opinions and our own baggage of our past. Most of us were taught early on not to trust a certain kind of person. All of us have built in us a certain kind of value system. Many Christians think it's not important to accept people from other backgrounds. If we are honest, all of us struggle at times with accepting people who are different from us. It is hard to relate to someone who is different from us. How do we accept other Christians who look different than us, and who worship different than us?

Let's read verse 7: *"Accept one another, then, just as Christ accepted you, in order to bring praise to God."* Accept one another. To accept others, we must first look at *why* we should accept one another. We are formed together out of "love" in Christ. As Christians, we adopt the same view of the world as Christ.

Let's turn to Philippians 2:1-5: "If you have any encouragement from being united with Christ, if any comfort from his love, if any fellowship with the Spirit, if any tenderness and compassion, then make my joy complete by being like-minded, having the same love, being one in spirit and purpose. Do nothing out of selfish ambition or vain conceit, but in humility consider others better than yourselves. Each of you should look not only to your own interests, but also to the interests of others. Your attitude should be the same as that of Christ Jesus." Most of us live to make a good impression on others and to fulfill our own pleasures. Accepting others creates unity. Caring for others creates unity.

Loving others creates unity. Putting others first demonstrates unity. Verse 3 here says, if there's anything that can destroy a person or a church, it is selfish ambition. **Selfish ambition destroys. Genuine humility builds.** To be humble and live humbly requires us to consider the interests of others as important as our own because Christ did.

How do we consider others better than our self? Galatians 5:25-26 tells us, "Since we live by the Spirit, let us keep in step with the Spirit. Let us not become conceited, provoking and envying each other." This provides us with a clear example of how we are to do the impossible. "Let us keep step with the Spirit." The key here is the idea of walking with the Spirit of the Lord. People who must tell you how good they are and always want recognition become conceited and have difficulty loving others. It's hard to put others before yourself when you are consumed with your own personal problems and issues.

If we are sons and daughters of the Lord, we are guaranteed the Holy Spirit as our approval. We need no approval from people. Philippians 2:4: "Each of you should look not only to your own interests, but also to the interests of others." Paul encourages us to guard ourselves against selfishness, prejudice, and jealousy, which could lead to dissension. If we show a genuine interest in others, we have made a positive step toward maintaining unity in the church. Philippians 2:5 says, "Your attitude should be the same as that of Christ Jesus." What kind of attitude did Christ have?

1) **Loving:** Jesus chose to have the attitude of love. (John 13:34-45)

2) **Humble:** Jesus shows us how to practice humility. (John 13:14-15)

3) **Willing to Serve:** Jesus became a servant. (Matthew 10:45)

Jesus was the perfect example of a loving, humble servant. When we die, wouldn't it be cool if our families could write on our gravestones, "He was a loving, humble servant." That would be the best legacy a person could leave. Oftentimes we view success as accomplishments, wealth, and power. These were virtues that Jesus did not consider as spiritual virtues. Jesus viewed love, humility, and service to others as his worldview. What is your view of the world? Is it possible to consider aligning your view with the way Christ sees the world?

CHAPTER 62
WHAT IT TAKES TO BE A MAXIMUM MAN
Romans 15:14

"I myself am convinced, my brothers, that you yourselves are full of goodness, complete in knowledge and competent to instruct one another."- Romans 15:14

This chapter deals with the boldness of the Apostle Paul. Paul begins to close his letter here in chapter 15. As we know, Paul had never been to Rome, but he provided the Church of Rome with his writings as a theological road map, or, should I say, a self-help manual of how to live the Christian life. Have you ever known anyone to be bold? Some might think of men like Winston Churchill, Martin Luther King, or Abe Lincoln, for example. For me, the boldest human to ever live was the Apostle Paul. He lived a bold and courageous life. He lived boldly and he wrote boldly.

Turn to 2 Corinthians 12. Let's read the section about all the difficult times Paul had. If you were given a compliment, what would be a compliment to you? What I believe to be a huge compliment for us, as Christians, is in verse 14: "I myself am convinced, my brothers, that you yourselves are full of goodness, complete in knowledge and competent to instruct one another." **I want to be a Maximum Man.** Paul epitomizes what it takes to be a Maximum Man. I want to be precise and to the point. Verse 14 outlines for us three specific areas of life that we must work on for us to be the man or Maximum Man God wants us to be:

1) **A Maximum Man is "full of goodness."** To be full of goodness, we must be of Godly character. The Holy Spirit, as we know, is key and fundamental to us receiving the power to live a holy life. But prior to the Holy Spirit entering our lives we must be submissive to the divine will of God. Being full of goodness is an external expression of an internal action. "Full of

goodness" means we, as sinners, are not perfect, but we allow Christ, who is perfect, to dominate our lives. What Paul is saying here is in order to become Maximum Men, we must be full of the goodness of Christ. To be "full of goodness" means to treat everyone with respect because we have respect for Christ. We received the "goodness" by God's grace through faith. We cannot boast of our goodness because it's because of God that we have the goodness. Ephesians 2:8 says, "For it is by grace you have been saved, through faith—and this not from yourselves, it is the gift of God." Where does goodness come from? Our goodness comes from God's workmanship. Every ounce of goodness in our souls comes from God and God alone. Since we are created in Jesus Christ, we are capable of doing good works because of His goodness.

2) **A Maximum Man must "be complete in knowledge."** What does it mean to be complete in knowledge? Not general knowledge, but deep knowledge of God's truth. Where does true, complete knowledge come from? Colossians 2:2-3 says, "My purpose is that they may be encouraged in heart and united in love, so that they may have the full riches of complete understanding, in order that they may know the mystery of God, namely, Christ, in whom are hidden all the treasures of wisdom and knowledge." To be a Maximum Man requires us to know with clarity, to know with certainty, to know without question that Christ is our power source. Christ is the source of power, the Holy Spirit is the pump that drives the power, and the Holy Spirit works to teach, purify, guide, and direct us. Before we can be complete in knowledge, we must first have a desire to know more about God. We must pray…**"God give me the desire to know you."** To become the man God wants us to be is to know God and be complete in knowledge. The completion of knowledge is deeper than answering all

the questions about God and it's more than knowing about God and all his attributes. To be complete in knowledge requires us to live out what we know. If we fail to live it out we have not completed the knowledge process.

3) **A Maximum Man must be "competent to instruct one another."** (Romans 15:14) We will never be all God wants us to be until we're able to teach others how to live the Christian life. A sign of maturity is when you have trained someone else to teach others to multiply themselves. The word "competent" in Greek means "to advise, counsel, teach, encourage." Every person who is a believer needs to be competent to instruct another person. Paul is pointing to the life of Christ. He is duplicating, in a way, the Great Commission in Matthew 28:19, which tells us to go make disciples. There is nothing we can do that is more important than investing our lives into other people. All of us can fuss about the government, what they do, what they don't do. There are those who want Obama to succeed and those who want him to fail. There are those who love Bush, and those who hate Bush. At the end of the day, we have to ask ourselves the question: "If every Christian spent the same amount of time investing their life in the life of someone else, as they did talking about politics, what kind of world would we have?" If we start with one Christian today, and he discipled another person for a year, and that person did the same thing, using geometric multiplication, how long would it take to win the population of the world? 37 years. 6.5 billion people would be discipled in 37 years if all believers fulfilled the Great Commission. To be a Maximum Man, God wants us to start discipling others. He wants us to be competent to instruct one another. Will you commit to expressing to others what Christ has done for you? Will you allow God to bring to you another person

to share what you know about God? Will you invest your life in the life of another person? When you do, you are being the Maximum Man God wants you to be.

CHAPTER 63
WHAT REAL MEN BRAG ABOUT
Romans 15:17-19

"Therefore I glory in Christ Jesus in my service to God."
- Romans 15:17

Have you ever been around a person who loved to brag about what they were able to accomplish? All of us love to enlighten others about our accomplishments. I used to know a guy years ago who always had a better story. If you caught a seven-pound bass, he caught a nine-pound bass. If you killed an eight-point, 175 lb. white-tailed deer, he killed a 10-point, 190 lb. white-tailed deer. He loved to brag. The reality is that, as humans, we all love to brag. The way you can tell if a guy is bragging is he starts out most of his sentences with "I." "I" ran 10 miles, "I" read the Bible five times, "I" won 22 people to the Lord on a mission trip, "I" am a deacon, "I," "I," "I." At the end of the day, what does "I" really mean? It's all about me. When things become about us, we put ourselves before others. When we brag about ourselves, it is a sign of insecurity. Insecurity comes when there is a gap between who we are and who we want others to think we are.

In my younger years, I played high school and college football. Every day my running-back coach would tell us to stay low. Everything we did, we did "low." If you have to block a huge guy, stay low. If you were tackling someone, stay low. The same goes for our life in Christ. When you get a better position in your job, stay low. When you become wealthy, stay low. When you go too high is when you might get knocked out. A secure person takes a lowly position about life. Be humble in the Lord and God will bless your life.

Here's a question for you today. What do real men brag about? Galatians 6:14 says, "May I never boast except in the cross of our Lord Jesus Christ, through which the world has been

271

crucified to me, and I to the world." Paul says "I will brag, but it will be about Jesus Christ." What would happen if we stopped bragging about ourselves and started bragging about what the Lord has done for us? It would radically change the way people view the world. 1 Corinthians 1:21 says, "Therefore, as it is written: 'Let him who boasts boast in the Lord.'" 2 Corinthians 10:17-18 says, "But, 'Let him who boasts boast in the Lord.'" For it is not the one who commends himself who is approved, but the one whom the Lord commends."

Let me say this: Be careful how you recognize and brag on people. Public recognition for donations and performance-based activities is dangerous because it leads to inflated pride and a skewed view of Christianity. We should reward the faithful, not those who give a lot of money. Unfortunately, the church has migrated toward rewarding the same person as the world rewards. The scary part is that we don't see anything wrong with it. We will never go wrong if we brag about the Lord. Recognition causes jealousy among others. Paul says if we are going to boast, if we're going to brag, brag on the Lord. When we seek the praise of people, we demand recognition. When we seek the praise of God, we boast about Him. What should we do when we receive praise? Give the credit to God. Never touch God's glory. 2 Corinthians 12:5 says, "I will boast about a man like that, but I will not boast about myself, except about my weaknesses." Romans 15:17-19 says, "Therefore I glory in Christ Jesus in my service to God. I will not venture to speak of anything except what Christ has accomplished through me in leading the Gentiles to obey God by what I have said and done by the power of signs and miracles, through the power of the Spirit. So from Jerusalem all the way around to Illyricum, I have fully proclaimed the gospel of Christ." Paul outlines five things about being a faithful leader:

1) **Never take credit for yourself.** Always use the opportunity to brag on God. An insecure man brags on himself. A secure man brags on God. (Psalm 86:13)

2) **Be obedient to the Lord.** Christ calls us to faith in Him, but He also calls us to obey Him. We are known through our love and measured by our obedience. (2 John 1:6)

3) **Maintain personal integrity.** Live your life the way you teach your kids. What we do speaks louder than what we say. (Proverbs 11:3)

4) **Affirmation of the power of the Sprit.** When we are teaching soundly, we will be led by the Spirit. (Romans 8:14)

5) **Complete the task.** Every person has a task. The main task for all of us is to live out the full gospel. Most guys want to "teach." For the most part, teaching is one-sided. Teaching is when I do all the talking and you do all the listening. Most of us have too much teacher in us. We want to tell someone what to do. Jesus told us not to teach, but to "go make disciples." To disciple changes the formula from I talk, you listen, to we both talk and we both listen. Disciple-making requires "life on life". It becomes a holistic approach to growing a person in the Lord. We interact in all aspects of life. Teachers say, "Let me tell you how to fish;" disciples say, "Let me fish with you." 100% of all preachers preach, but only about 10% of all preachers preach *and* disciple. We have plenty of people telling others what to do, but what we really need is people willing to show others what to do and how to do it (Acts 20:24).

CHAPTER 64
LIVING A LIFE IN THE SPIRIT
Romans 15:23-33

"I urge you, brothers, by our Lord Jesus Christ and by the love of the Spirit, to join me in my struggle by praying to God for me."
- Romans 15:30

Paul wrote the major part of this letter to the Roman Church as a means to explain the Biblical doctrines. As we come to the end of chapter 15, we find that Paul is seeking to express himself on a more personal level. He talks about how he wants to minister to the people and fellowship with them. This passage gives us a clear picture of how he forged these profound principles in his life. Paul's focus was on the will of God.

Verse 32 says, *"So that by God's will I may come to you with joy and together with you be refreshed."* Paul followed the model provided for him by Christ. John 5:30 says, "By myself I can do nothing; I judge only as I hear, and my judgment is just, for I seek not to please myself but him who sent me." Let me ask you a question: How do we follow God's will for our life? There's only one way. **To be led by the Holy Spirit. If we are led by God's Spirit, we will be in His will.** Many people say they want to find God's will for their life. The first step of finding God's will is to be led by His Spirit. You will find God's will for your life if you're willing to be led by the Spirit of God.

God's Spirit produces God's will. There is no way possible if we're full of the Holy Spirit that we can be outside the will of God. Acts 16:6-10 says, "But the Spirit of God did not permit them." We must understand that we are exposed to the influence of two powers: The power of Satan and the power of God. There is no other power. We must come to the conclusion in life that any power outside of God is clearly Satan. This is a difficult concept to comprehend. You mean if I believe in myself

275

outside of God's power that I'm under the control of Satan? Exactly.

I want us to focus on the subject matter today of the Holy Spirit. Turn to Acts 1:5: "For John baptized with water, but in a few days you will be baptized with the Holy Spirit." The baptism of the Holy Spirit must be understood in every part of the Christian life. We cannot belong to Christ without His Spirit (Romans 8:9). God's Spirit unites us. God's Spirit empowers us. God's Spirit guides us. God's Spirit is the power of our new life. The Holy Spirit is constantly changing our lives as we become more like Him.

Galatians 3:3 says, "Are you so foolish? After beginning with the Spirit, are you now trying to attain your goal by human effort?" Our growth in Christ comes from living and walking in the Spirit of God. Our growth is due to God's redemptive work in us by the power of His Holy Spirit. Much too often we try to follow our plan. Our plan is filled with self. It is consumed with making us look good. God's plan is when we are led by His Spirit. God's plan is filled with serving others, not our self. God's plan is consumed with making God look good because He lives in us. He controls us. His plan will never be focused on us looking good. Here's how that works. People are composed of three elements:

1) **Body/Flesh:** The temporary body we inhabit while on earth.

2) **Soul:** Our volition or character. Our soul ultimately filters all the decisions we make.

3) **Spirit:** Our connection to God. Our spirit is activated only when we are in a personal relationship with Christ. When that happens, we gain direct access to God through the Holy Spirit.

Here's my question to you: Will you take the risk to give your life fully over to Him? Will you give your life over to God and let the Spirit of God lead, guide, and direct your life?

CHAPTER 65

PERSONAL GREETING
Romans 16:1-16

"Greet one another with a holy kiss. All the churches of Christ send greetings. "- Romans 16:16

If you are writing a letter to a dear friend whom you've not seen for a long time, and you're coming to a close in the letter, you would generally express yourself with a deep sense of gratitude. This passage is the most extensive and intimate expression of love and appreciation ever recorded by Paul. The Book of Romans is a very popular book; however, chapter 16 is often overlooked by preachers, teachers, and Bible students. This chapter offers very little explicit teaching. Paul uses this time to recognize many of his Christian brothers in Christ. While we know very little about most of these people, through his words, we see the heart of the person.

What is the most important part of a person? The most important part of a person is his heart. The heart of a person reflects the character of a person. Turn to 1 Samuel 16:6-7, "When they arrived, Samuel saw Eliab and thought, 'Surely the LORD's anointed stands here before the LORD.' But the LORD said to Samuel, 'Do not consider his appearance or his height, for I have rejected him. The LORD does not look at the things man looks at. Man looks at the outward appearance, but the LORD looks at the heart.'" The heart of a man is at the core of who he is. King Saul was a tall, handsome, and impressive man. Samuel, the prophet, appeared to be looking for a similar man to replace Saul. Most of us judge by appearance, but God looks at what's inside. The thing we need to do is to be able to see what God sees. A person's appearance does not reveal what they are really like or what their core values are in life. What is it that God really looks at? Faith and character. You see, God has the advantage because He can see everything on the inside of us. We cannot see inside, but we can see is what's on the outside, or the evidence of the

Spirit in our lives. The evidence of the Spirit reveals Himself through our actions. Turn to Galatians 5:22: "But the fruit of the Spirit is love, joy, peace, patience, kindness, goodness, faithfulness."

Now, let's read Romans 16:1-16: *"I commend to you our sister Phoebe, a deacon of the church in Cenchreae. I ask you to receive her in the Lord in a way worthy of his people and to give her any help she may need from you, for she has been the benefactor of many people, including me. Greet Priscilla and Aquila, my co-workers in Christ Jesus. They risked their lives for me. Not only I but all the churches of the Gentiles are grateful to them. Greet also the church that meets at their house. Greet my dear friend Epenetus, who was the first convert to Christ in the province of Asia. Greet Mary, who worked very hard for you. Greet Andronicus and Junia, my fellow Jews who have been in prison with me. They are outstanding among the apostles, and they were in Christ before I was. Greet Ampliatus, my dear friend in the Lord. Greet Urbanus, our co-worker in Christ, and my dear friend Stachys. Greet Apelles, whose fidelity to Christ has stood the test. Greet those who belong to the household of Aristobulus. Greet Herodion, my fellow Jew. Greet those in the household of Narcissus who are in the Lord. Greet Tryphena and Tryphosa, those women who work hard in the Lord. Greet my dear friend Persis, another woman who has worked very hard in the Lord. Greet Rufus, chosen in the Lord, and his mother, who has been a mother to me, too. Greet Asyncritus, Phlegon, Hermes, Patrobas, Hermas and the other brothers and sisters with them. Greet Philologus, Julia, Nereus and his sister, and Olympas and all the Lord's people who are with them. Greet one another with a holy kiss. All the churches of Christ send greetings."*

I believe Paul saw the things God saw in every person mentioned in the closing portion of Romans. He did not see inside the heart, but he saw the by-product of the heart. I believe every person Paul names was an example of what God's Spirit produces. **What's in the well will always come up in the bucket.** For you intellectuals that don't understand the concept, it's this: What's on the inside will always come to the outside when put under pressure. If you want to really see what's inside a person's heart, put them under stress and pressure and you will discover who they really are in their weakness. We must follow and believe Paul's words in Galatians 5:16: "So I say, live by the Spirit, and you will not gratify the desires of the sinful nature." We all have a sinful nature, we all have sinful desires, and we all have thoughts that are impure. Before we can be led by the Spirit, we must crucify all the baggage we have. It must be totally given over to the Lord. God's Spirit cannot reside where there is intense sin. If we ignore such sins and refuse to deal with them, it's a sign that the Spirit does not reside in us.

This is where I'm really trying to go. It should be our goal in life, not to try to become "someone" and be popular, but to be someone who is filled with the love of God, has the joy of the Lord in our heart, always keeps a level head because of our peace in Christ, has patience in the Lord, has a kind heart, is never hurtful, displays goodness, is faithful and dependable, is gentle and not overbearing, is not selfish, and is full of self-control. The Spirit produces these character traits in us. All of these traits are directly out of the heart of Christ. The only way for us to have these traits is to be under His control. We cannot obtain these traits our self, but if we want to grow into these traits, we must connect our life to His life. He must be the object of our love. We must know Him, love Him, imitate Him, respect Him, and honor Him in all of our ways. What is it in your life that has not been fully crucified? Unforgiveness, bitterness, hatred, jealously, rage, lust, selfishness, drunkenness, envy, or orgies? I believe there was a time when everyone named in Paul's greetings had to deal with one or more of these issues. Only when they trusted Christ and asked Him to complete the work in them were they able to walk in the Spirit. Will you get personal with Christ? Will you let Christ enter into the depths of your heart and restore you with His power and grace?

CHAPTER 66
WATCH OUT FOR
SLICK-TALKING PREACHERS
Romans 16:17-27

"I urge you, brothers, to watch out for those who cause divisions and put obstacles in your way that are contrary to the teaching you have learned. Keep away from them."- Romans 16:17

The conclusion of our study of Romans leaves us with some key points to consider. First, we should be careful of those who are not teaching the true gospel. The world is but a fog. It's hard for us to see beyond deceptive and slick-talking orators of the day. Paul tells us to be careful.

Verse 17: *"I urge you, brothers, to watch out for those who cause divisions and put obstacles in your way that are contrary to the teaching you have learned. Keep away from them."* Every church has those who cause dissension. Most of the time when a person is divisive it means they have a difficult time with authority. Love forgives all evil, but love does not condone or ignore evil. Paul is coming to a close in his letter to the Church of Rome and finds it necessary to insert this caution. Titus 3:9 says, "But avoid foolish controversies and genealogies and arguments and quarrels about the law, because these are unprofitable and useless." We are to shun foolish controversies. 2 Timothy 2:23 says, "Don't have anything to do with foolish and stupid arguments, because you know they produce quarrels." We are to refuse foolish and ignorant arguments. Paul is telling us to never let anyone undermine the teaching we have learned. So, I say the very same thing to you. Never let anyone undermine the gospel of Christ, and the love and grace that He has for all mankind. If anyone tries to do so, walk away. Don't argue; denounce them, and move on. Anyone who does not recognize God's truths and reflect Christ as the model is not of the love of God.

Verse 25: *"Now to him who is able to establish you by my gospel and the proclamation of Jesus Christ, according to the revelation of the mystery hidden for long ages past..."* The Book of Romans ends with a doxology – praising God for what He has done through the Son of God. Paul recognizes and celebrates the power of the gospel. The gospel is established in the truth of God by the power of the Holy Spirit. The gospel proclaims Christ. In 1 Corinthians 4:5-6, Paul says, "We do not preach about ourselves, but about Christ Jesus, as Lord." If we live according to the gospel of Christ, God will bless our life with the following:

Romans 3:22: Righteousness comes by faith in Christ.

Romans 3:24: Justification comes by His grace through redemption.

Romans 4:24: Righteousness is given to those who believe in Christ.

Romans 5:1: We receive peace with God through our Lord, Jesus Christ.

Romans 6:8: By dying with Christ, we will also live with Christ.

Romans 6:23: The free gift of eternal life comes through Jesus Christ, our Lord.

Romans 7:6: We are able to serve in the newness of the Spirit.

Romans 8:14: We are led by the Spirit.

Romans 8:16: The Spirit is our witness that we are His children.

Romans 8:39: We cannot be separated from the love of God.

This man called Jesus is a life-changing, revolutionary guy who has more love, grace, and mercy for us than we will ever know. He offers hope, peace, and love. Regardless of who we are, there are a couple of things we all have in common: Everyone needs support and everyone needs to be loved. We cannot function without these two vital aspects or basic requirements of life. Most of us are faced with the ultimate question: What do I do with Christ? Jesus is far more than we could ever imagine. If we seek Him, we will find Him. If we put Him on the shelf, He will do us no good. Jesus can only fully function when He has received permission to have full and total access to our life. Jesus wants to be in control of us. Will you let Christ become the Lord of your life?

The Book of Romans leads us all to a point of self-examination and commitment. To be the person God wants you to be requires a response; it requires radical change in your thoughts, movements, actions, and way of life. To be the person God wants you to be causes you to take inventory of your own life so you can see how lost you are without Him. Will you let God transform, mold, and shape you into the person he wants you to be? If you do, you will experience a peace deep in your soul that very few people experience and God will grow your life into what He wants. My prayer for you is that you would make a commitment to the Lord today to live out the gospel and become all that God has made and called you to be.

Acknowledgments

When we are committed to following Jesus, we have all that He is alive in us. We are equipped by Him to face every challenge. By His grace, He also brings people into our lives to encourage us. I have been especially aware of this during the writing of this book. I want to say "thank you" to everyone who has faithfully supported me.

To my family – Paul, Emily, Wilder, Audra, Michael and Lizanne, thank you for your love, encouragement and great help in putting this book together. Special appreciation goes to Emily, who edited my writing and put things in the proper order, and to Audra, for her help in proofing the manuscript. My family is God's special blessing in my life.

To my Bible study class – The men in this class gave me the purpose for this book and prompted me to undertake the task of writing it. I love these faithful men and am indebted to them for their encouragement.

To Dr. Phillip Jett – This Godly man is my true friend and spiritual mentor. He has traveled with me on dozens of mission trips to Brazil. His love and leadership have been unwavering for over twenty-five years. Dr. Jett, thank you for your great support in the development of this book.

To Dr. Wade Akins – This friend and spiritual leader taught me how to "make disciples." Wade and his wife, Barbara, constantly travel around the world making disciples and training leaders. They are my heroes in the Faith, and their investment in me will always be treasured. I will never forget the ten years we spent together each summer on the mission field in Brazil.

To Eduardo and Rosanne Sores – These friends and ministry partners are faithful missionaries in Brazil. Daily, they live out the Gospel by making disciples, starting churches and feeding the poor. Eduardo I thank you for your leadership and love you have for people.

To my office staff – These vital assistants work beyond the call of duty. Michelle Warren, Ben Truex and Monica Austin, thank you for all that you have done to make this book a reality.

To Dr. Arthur David – This dear friend, who reads the scriptures at our Bible studies every Thursday morning, is a true follower of Christ. Dr. David is one of the most intelligent men I know and his love for God is shown in his life.

To Wayne Bristow – This friend has devoted his life to doing the work of the evangelist and serving the Lord. Wayne, I am grateful for your help in reviewing the material in this book.

To Micky Tabor – This friend is a true friend. He has walked with me through many obstacles in my life. I am grateful for his friendship.

To Pastor Willie Miles – This man has blessed my life with prayer and encouragement. He loves the Lord and has a passion to grow his church.

To Larry Jones – This friend has been an influence in the lives of many children. His encouragement and dedication to our weekly Bible study has been evident for the last six years.

Made in the USA
Charleston, SC
16 March 2014